CW00501639

# May I Borrow Your
# Eraser?

Daily Inspirational Meditations to Erase Misconceptions
Brought On By The Lies Of The Enemy

## VERA J. RIDEOUT

# DEDICATION

"It is with humble regards that I dedicate this book to my lifeline found in my children, Patrick, Corbin, and Arielle. Each day of my life, God allowed you to keep me focused on living a life pleasing to God and well worth you emulating. I wasn't perfect but you loved me anyway and never complained, even when I needed God's eraser time and time again. Thank you for your constant support. God's grace and favor be with you always. I love you."

*Momma*

# FOREWORD

In every generation, God raises up a group of people who love Him and those whom Christ Jesus died for. They have continual experiences with Him in His Presence as they seek to know Him intimately. They learn His Voice, discover His ways, and Character. They surrender to His Kingdom Processes for their lives, that He might "make them" for His glory.

Vera Rideout is one from this group. She has made it her life's pursuit to walk with the King of Glory in order to be a praise to the glory of His grace. In doing so she has discovered the wonders of His love, mercy, and His grace. She has had the privilege to see them through the eyes of a school teacher and an educator.

"May I Borrow Your Eraser" is a wonderful expression of the depth of God's love and mercy for mankind. As you read this book, you'll go on this wonderful journey through the landscape of God's heart, discovering along the way that His Hand is stretched out to you, granting you another chance to live life as He originally meant for you to live.

The costly Blood of Jesus Christ can wipe away everything written in your life that God didn't originally write for your life. His Love, Grace, and Mercy combined is the Eraser. Receive your "Fresh Start" today!

Apostle Craig Banks

Senior Pastor, Canaan Christian Center, Pine Bluff, Arkansas
Chief Apostle, Canaan Apostolic Covering, Pine Bluff, Arkansas

# INTRODUCTION

We all carry things from our past that we want to put behind us. There is good news! Suffering the humility of the cross for us, Jesus reconciled and redeemed us back into the royal priesthood of God's Kingdom. Hence, today we stand as kings and priests, clothed in righteousness, washed in His blood, and all stains of sins past, present, and future erased. Jesus erased the stain of sin and everything associated with it. Through the written word of God, we can take the pages of our lives that have lies from the enemy encrypted on each page and change the content of what shall come next. God's word is our personal eraser. When we borrow God's eraser, it allows us to rewrite the story He has predestined for each of us to live. Go ahead, borrow His eraser! It's life changing. Together we will dive into 99 days of daily inspiration to erase the misconceptions brought on by the enemy's lies. I hope that you will take every bit of truth from each of these devotions and go to war with them against the enemy. You are a beloved child of God and whom the Son sets free is free indeed. Doubt, fear, unbelief, depression, anxiety, low self-esteem and so much more will be erased by the word of God and the powerful name of Jesus!

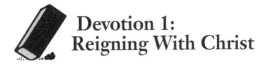 # Devotion 1:
## Reigning With Christ

*"Having disarmed principalities and powers, He made a public spectacle of them, triumphing over them in it."*

Colossians 2:15

Great are You, Lord and greatly to be praised. Father, You reign! Because He reigns so do we. Have you ever looked at the struggle you're in and identified it as "my struggle"? Actually, the struggle doesn't belong to you. It belongs to the devil. The devil wants you to take ownership of the struggle but it belongs to him. You see, Satan is the one with the issues.

We've been redeemed by the blood of the Lamb. He knows that. In actuality, he is fighting for his life to be lived through yours. Therefore, the devil produces chaos, calamity, and hatred so that he can draw you into his world away from the protection of the reigning King, Jesus. It is not going to happen anymore. You must tell him emphatically, "No! No way, no how! Jesus is my Lord and He is your Lord too! I did not stutter, Jesus is Lord of all, including you, Satan. Get up out of here! I reign with Jesus as both king and priest."

Of course, the devil does not want to hear it but he must take heed and do what you have declared. After all, he was stripped of his dominion by the reigning King, Jesus! Hallelujah! The devil will leave and all his followers must go with him. Great are You, Lord and greatly to be praised! Father, You reign and as Your child, so do I! Amen!

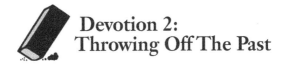

# Devotion 2:
# Throwing Off The Past

*"Casting all your care upon Him, for He cares for you."*

1 Peter 5:7

On Thursday, many of my Facebook friends will post a status that's referred to as "Throwback Thursday." In the status there's usually a photo of something from the past. This photo is generally a reminder of a pleasant period from their past. It often includes family, friends, neighbors and associates. Today, I want to give you a chance to "throw" but not a throwback. I want to encourage you to cast away the things of the past so that you can move into the future.

Hence, on this "Throw-away Thursday", we're pulling off the blinders of deception, peeling away the layers of rejection, flushing out the falsehoods of satanic delusions and pushing open the closed doors of unbelief. Once this is done, we're casting every care that's associated with the powers of darkness onto the Savior of the world once and for all.

Our Father has made provision for us to be free of the negativity associated with the bondage we've been under. Actually, we're free from all stigmas of bondage. We're free from the ruler of sin because the

Master of All defeated him for us. Glory be to God! We're free! Hallelujah! No longer bound! No more sin holding us! Shout unto God with a voice of triumph! Praise the Lord!

So on this Throw-Away Thursday gather all the heaviness (cares and weights) of sin bondage and cast them upon the Savior! Put on instead the garment of praise! Praise is our weapon!

Other Verses: Isaiah 61:3, Psalm 8:2

 # Devotion 3:
# Perfect Peace

*"You will keep him in perfect peace, whose mind is stayed on You, because he trusts in You."*

Isaiah 26:3

To the One who sits on the throne be all blessing, glory, honor, majesty, power, and dominion forever! There's only One who receives all our praise. There's but One deserving of our worship. He alone is God. Today to abide in perfect peace, we keep our mind stayed on Him. Hallelujah to the one true and living God. Forevermore unto thee, our God do we lift our voice in adoration of Your faithfulness. Forever Amen!

Other Verses: Revelation 5:13

 # Devotion 4:
# Living Word

*"For the word of God is living and powerful, and sharper than any two-edged sword, piercing even to the division of soul and spirit, and of joints and marrow, and is a discerner of the thoughts and intents of the heart."*

Hebrews 4:12

Most people have a favorite quote or saying. What's yours? Is it a scripture you memorized as a child or a line from a poem you rehearsed in high school? Maybe it's a quote from your favorite book or movie? No matter from whence it originated, it inspires you to do good, raises the bar of your personal expectations or just makes you feel all warm and fuzzy inside.

When you think of or say your quote, you do so with confidence. And now, the rest of the story. The words you speak are conducive to your personal growth and development. Their origination must be from the thoughts that are pure, lovely and of good report. Dwelling on bloops and blunders you've made will not produce thoughts or speech that is for your best interest. We've all failed at some point in our lives.

Yet, our failures are forgiven because of the life that was given for us by Christ Jesus on Calvary. Our errors and the errs of all mankind past, present, and future are under the blood of Jesus. Isn't that enough to cause you to speak with confidence of His goodness and mercy toward you?

Everybody has something to say about the condition of our nation and world, but when will we say what the Word of God says? God has given man dominion over the earth. It's in our authority to call those things that aren't, as if they were. When we stop promoting hatred and negativity and start applying the principles we claim to stand on, which are Christ-centered, we'll see a change in society.

When we humble ourselves before God, we'll see the frailty of man. When we come before Him in prayer, we'll receive directions to change the worlds in which we have influence. When we turn from the wickedness of the evil at hand, and seek God's face, He'll hear us. One by one as we do our part, our world's condition shall change. I admonish you to season your speech with the salt of God's word. Salt preserves, but on an open wound it irritates before the outward healing begins.

It is "The Word" and not just any word that will restore us to God's righteous way of thinking and living. The Word that is alive and active in each of us is more than capable of restoring our society to the truths on which it was founded, the truth of God's Word. Finally, as you quote today, speak life by using words that bring God's way of living to life.

Other Verses: 2 Chronicles 7:14, Philippians 4:8-9

# Devotion 5:
# I Am

*"Therefore God also has highly exalted Him and given Him the name which is above every name, that at the name of Jesus every knee should bow, of those in heaven, and of those on earth, and of those under the earth, and that every tongue should confess that Jesus Christ is Lord, to the glory of God the Father."*

Philippians 2:9-11

In the midst of what you're going through, stop accentuating the devil's position. Say nothing else to him and instead talk to the Lord Jesus. You see when you say to Jesus the words, "You are" followed by what He is to you, Jesus responds, "I Am" what you just told Him He was, because he is who you have professed Him to be.

Jesus lives in you, so nothing can by any means harm you. Let me make this so clear that even a blind man can see: Anything that has a name must (I didn't stutter. I said MUST!) bow to the Name above all names. That name is Jesus. So no matter what you're going through, call on the name above all names, then stand still and see the salvation of the Lord! The Great I Am speaks loud and clear. Listen to His voice. He is everything you want and all that you need. Praise the name of Jesus!

 **Devotion 6:
Not Forgotten**

*"God is not a man, that He should lie, nor a son of man,
that He should repent. Has He said, and will He not
do? Or has He spoken, and will He not make it good?
Behold, I have received a command to bless;
He has blessed, and I cannot reverse it."*

Numbers 23:19-20

P raise be unto our Lord and Savior for He's
given everything that is associated with life and
godliness. There's no failure in Him. So let me
encourage you to know this one thing. If it appears
that you've prayed and prayed and the situation hasn't
changed, the table hasn't turned, the circumstances
have gotten worse, you're still stuck in a rut, or if you're
just hovering in space, none of these seemingly delays
or detours mean God has forgotten or failed you.

There is no failure in God! Instead you've been
in a process of development. You've been in a place
of protection. You've been in a season of change even
though you saw nothing changing. Today ask the Lord,
"Show me a glimpse of my future." Just a glimpse will
be enough to let you know emphatically that you've
not been forsaken. So, my challenge to you, ask and
you'll get an answer. Seek Him and you're surely find

Him. Knock at His door and it shall be opened.

The Lord seeks those who call out to Him. He desires those whose heart is toward Him. He rewards those who diligently seek Him. Truth is, He can do anything but forsake or fail you. Call upon Him. He's near. As you cry out to Him, He's attentive to your cry. He'll show you great and mighty things in your life that you have no idea of! If you can but believe and receive, on this day, receive the word of truth. Jesus has not forgotten nor has He failed you. The blessing still reigns in your life today. To God be the Glory! Amen.

# Devotion 7:
# Daily Ministry

*"His lord said to him, Well done, good and faithful servant; you have been faithful over a few things, I will make you ruler over many things. Enter into the joy of your lord.'"*

Matthew 25:23

Many of us go to a place of employment each day. Some of us own and operate our own businesses. Some of us have been in the same profession for many years. Others have been in the workforce long enough to retire. Now retirement has become the daily routine. Today, I wish to pose a few questions for you to ponder, speaking both to those in the workforce and those who are retired.

As you go or went to your "job", was there ever a time you saw it as a place of an opportunity for ministry? Out of all the time you spend or spent at your workplace, did you make the most of it? Did you utilize the teachings of Christ so that God's glory can be or could have been seen by others through you? If you never quoted a scripture or made a verbal reference to our Father would those in your sphere of influence recognize that you are a child of God? Could they or can they tell just by the life they see or saw each day you were present?

I pose these questions because people of the world search for miracles, signs, and wonders and some of the greatest can be found in our everyday lives. As we exemplify the life of the risen Savior, we show God to the world. Our daily responses to a heart's cry, a seemingly meager need, and a brutish attitude reflects the response of the one who died for us.

Do we give true representation of Him as the light of the world? Do they only see our own selfish response rather than viewing everything through the eyes of Christ? When we see our "job" as the ministry field, we'll work more productively towards the saving of souls. When we see our daily tasks as ministry, we'll come to realize that the real payday comes when we're standing before the master. The final payment is made as He says, "Well done, good and faithful servant; thou hast been faithful over a few things, I will make thee ruler over many things: enter thou into the joy of thy lord. Come, ye blessed of my Father, inherit the kingdom prepared for you from the foundation of the world."

The benefits of a "job" stretch beyond a paycheck. Often it is seen in the eyes of the destitute, the smile of the downtrodden, the joy of one given a second chance or the embrace of the neglected and overlooked. Yet, we'll miss these benefits if we only see or saw our job as work and not as ministry.

Other Verses: Matthew 25:34, 2 Corinthians 5:14, 20

# Devotion 8:
# Forgiveness

*"For if you forgive men their trespasses, your heavenly Father will also forgive you. But if you do not forgive men their trespasses, neither will your Father forgive your trespasses."*

Matthew 6:14-15

Just one last note on the topic of forgiveness. Before we were formed in our mothers' wombs, Christ gave His life for the sins. He took on the sin weight of the whole world so that we could undeniably be reconciled back into right standing with our Father.

Have you ever been in physical pain? Was it pleasant? Did you pray that the pain would never end? No! You cried out for relief. Jesus could have pleaded for His life while on the cross but instead He pleaded for the lives of those who nailed Him to the cross. His nature of love was to ask for their forgiveness.

Yet, I choose to believe that in His words of, "Father, forgive them for they know not what they do." there is a deeper context. These immortal words spanned whole generations of the lives of men then, now, and are yet to come. His statement resounds throughout history until His imminent soon and coming return for His people. Let not unforgiveness whether you're dead or alive, you fail to be "caught up to meet Him."

Grace is given to us to forgive.

So we pray, "...and forgive us our trespasses as we forgive those who trespass against us." Remember to whom much has been given, much is required.

Other Verses: Luke 12:48

# Devotion 9:
# God Is Love

*"So God created man in His own image; in the image of God He created him; male and female He created them."*

Genesis 1:27

Let's hang out here one more day. There's a reason. Only the nature of God which is love can combat and give you victory over unforgiveness. Love, love, love. Love sets us free. Jesus died so that you and I could love perfectly. We were created in the image of God. We have all the attributes He has. His most dominate attribute is love. Sin caused us to override the dominate trait of love we received from Him.

Through the death, burial, and resurrection of Christ Jesus to love without strings attached, expectation of anything in return, or out of obligation was returned to us. There is no price for us to pay to love. Jesus paid the price in full. We owe no leftover balance, shipping, interest or hidden costs. Our ability to love comes with the only stipulation of choice.

You'll find that when you choose to love, forgiveness finds the best seat in your heart and you begin to look at all people, circumstances, and situations from a different perspective. That new perspective is through the eyes of love. Once more ask God to show you whom you have laid a charge of unforgiveness against. Then choose to love them anyway. Release the charge. You're holding someone guilty because of offense but you're guilty of unforgiveness.

Before His death, Jesus prayed that we would be made one again in unity with He and the Father. Love is the binding agent that connects us both to the Father and to each other. Forgiveness is one of the many characteristics that demonstrates our connection to the Father. We are forgiven, so should we forgive. No longer live by a double standard. Live by the nature of God, the nature of love.

Other Verses: John 17:20-25

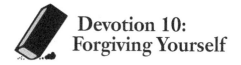 **Devotion 10:
Forgiving Yourself**

*"As far as the east is from the west, so far has He removed our
transgressions from us. As a father pities his children, so
the Lord pities those who fear Him. For He knows our
frame; He remembers that we are dust."*

Psalm 103:12-14

P reviously, I wrote about forgiveness and our need
to forgive. Helen Baylor sang a song entitled Sea
of Forgetfulness. This is the place all of our sins
have been placed in God's eyes. He doesn't remember
nor does He bring our past sins back up to us. He
forgave us once for everything we have done or ever
shall do. Forgiveness of our past mistakes now lies in
our hands. Release yourself of the unforgiveness you
hold against yourself. Set yourself free. Come on. Say
it, "I forgive me."

Some of you may need to be looking in the mirror
as you say this. You need to see the relief come across
your own face when you speak the words that bring
freedom and restoration to your own soul. 70 times 7
might just be the number of times you need for self-
preservation as you choose to forgive the offenses you
have toward yourself. Grace to forgive yourself is yours.
Believe it. Receive it. Set yourself free. Walk in liberty.

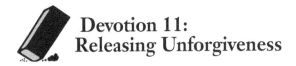 # Devotion 11:
# Releasing Unforgiveness

*"Let all bitterness, wrath, anger, clamor, and evil speaking be put away from you, with all malice. And be kind to one another, tenderhearted, forgiving one another, even as God in Christ forgave you."*

Ephesians 4:31-32

Forgiveness. We all need it. We all need to give it. Sometimes out of ignorance we hold grudges, malice or bitterness for years. All the while, building up sickness and disease in our bodies, and hatred in our hearts. The sad thing is that unforgiveness does more to destroy the one holding it than the one to who it is charged.

It is self-examination time. You don't need to go to the doctor for prescriptions nor to friends for their advice. Today this examination carries no co-pay or hidden costs. It's free and you cannot only make the diagnosis, but also begin immediate treatment to recover.

Look deep within. What do you see? Let go of any and all unforgiveness. I'm starting with me. I forgive myself for past mistakes both involuntarily made and those I knew full well what I was doing. Lord, I repent of not forgiving myself. Now I release any and all unforgiveness toward my family, friends, colleagues, neighbors and associates. Lord, I repent of not forgiving others. Let's walk out of this self-examination free of the sickness called unforgiveness.

Other Verses: Matthew 6:12; 6:14-15:18:21-22

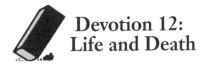 # Devotion 12:
## Life and Death

*"Death and life are in the power of the tongue,
and those who love it will eat its fruit."*

Proverbs 18:21

Trouble in your way? Tell it to move. Don't stress. Don't be anxious. Trouble has to move at your command. The diabolical plan of the enemy is to destroy your stamina, break your will, and destroy your focus. It shall not be so! Rise up and command this day to be what God ordained it to be.

Trouble be gone! At the sound of your words, trouble must cease and desist! What are you going to do? The power of life and death is in your tongue. You better tell what needs to live to live, and what needs to die to die! Stop wasting time! Open your mouth and decree the word of God over every situation that has troubled you. Yep! There may be some situations that are trouble makers but today you are the trouble breaker.

# Devotion 13:
# Time

*"...redeeming the time, because the days are evil."*

Ephesians 5:16

Moving about in a rush we sometimes forget the one thing that's most needed in our day to day hustle and bustle of life. Often we overlook this until it's too late to gain it back. Of course, we're remorseful that we didn't take advantage of the opportunity nor did we use it wisely. So we most often look back with regret and wish we'd had more of it or used it more wisely. The thing I'm referring to is time.

Time comes and goes but it's up to us to use it in a manner that is beneficial. Apostle Craig Banks has implied on more than one occasion, "God isn't short on land, riches, or laborers, but the one thing that's waning away is time" (paraphrased). So today, set your heart to redeem the lost time, while using the remaining time you have to impact your world of influence in the best way possible. Let this time be the time you leave a legacy of truth, servanthood, and righteousness. You've been given the grace to do so. Don't waste the time you have.

Other Verses: Psalm 39:4

# Devotion 14:
# Today

*"This is the day the Lord has made; We will rejoice and be glad in it."*

Psalm 118:23

Start the day with the blessed assurance that this day shall be a great day. It shall be filled with peace, prosperity and favor. It shall be a day of open doors and plentiful praise. You shall have everything you need. Your financial coffers shall be full and overflow. Endless bounty comes to you. It's the Lord's doing and it's marvelous in our eyes! Amen!

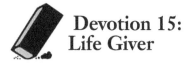 **Devotion 15:**
**Life Giver**

*"In my distress I called upon the Lord, and cried out to
my God; He heard my voice from His temple, and my cry
came before Him, even to His ears."*

Psalm 18:6

D id you know that you need the Lord today
just as much as you did the day you asked
Him into your life as Lord and Savior? God is
still your refuge. Run to Him. He is still your strength.
Draw from Him. He is still your peace. Cry out unto
Him. He is still your shield. Stay in His shadow. Our
Lord is still your answer. Ask of him.

As a baby, we were birthed into the world totally
dependent upon a caregiver to meet our every need.
Today, we are dependent upon a Life Giver who sustains
us through the blood of His risen Son. I tried Him and
I know him. There is no failure in Him. Having him in
my life has made the difference. Just having Him there.

All things work together for the good of those who
love the Lord! You know it's true! So together we pray.
Unto thee do we cry out, dear Lord. Attend unto our
cry. You alone are Lord! Blessed be Your name. Thank
you for receiving us as Your own. Be glorified both in
and through us. Amen! Amen!

# Devotion 16:
# Wonderfully Made

*"I will praise You, for I am fearfully and wonderfully made; Marvelous are Your works, and that my soul knows very well."*

Psalm 139:14

The beauty in life is in more than flora and fauna. You are the wonder that causes life to have essence. Recognize your value. Note your worth. See your contribution in life. You're worth so much more than you've given yourself credit. Yes, you are worth more than you believe. God's Son knew your importance before you were formed in your mother's womb.

God formed you in His image. Not the image of an angel but of Himself. Fearfully and wonderfully made are you. You may be imitated but you'll never be duplicated. You are God's poetry in motion and no one else has the rhythm that you move to. One of a kind, that's who you are. So recognize that life is better because of who you are. Love yourself and be yourself. God loves the you that He created to be like Him.

Other Verses: Genesis 1:27

# Devotion 17:
# A New Thing

*"Behold, I will do a new thing, now it shall spring forth;*
*Shall you not know it? I will even make a road in the*
*wilderness and rivers in the desert."*

Isaiah 43:19

The day has finally arrived! The time you thought would never get here has finally come! The confessions you've made are right before your eyes! The sacrifices you have made are reaping their harvest. You didn't know it would happen this way. You didn't think suddenly could actually mean immediately. In fact, you had almost forgotten the promises you had believed in for what seemed like ages. In God's sight it hasn't even been a day!

You're on track! This is happening in His timing! Oh, not without resistance, but most certainly with faith and perseverance! Glory to God! You've reached another level of prosperity and authority! What are you going to do now? Walk in it! Yes! That's the best you can do! You deserve it! It's yours! Act like you know that you know that you know, "Yep! It's my time!"

Other Verses: Isaiah 48:3

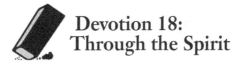

# Devotion 18:
# Through the Spirit

*"Abstain from every form of evil. Now may the God of peace Himself sanctify you completely; and may your whole spirit, soul, and body be preserved blameless at the coming of our Lord Jesus Christ."*

1 Thessalonians 5:22-23

God is a spirit. Man is created in God's image or likeness. We are a three part being: spirit, soul, and body. God made our spirit to be king over our soul and body. It is the spirit of man who has the ability to commune with God. Just as Adam communed with God, through our spirit, we too, can communicate with the Deity.

Our Father made our spirit to be king of the soul and body. The soul which includes our will, mind, intellect, emotions, and imagination, are to serve and obey our spirit. The body was made to be a slave to carry out the wishes of the spirit directed by the soul. Somewhere in the equation we got it twisted and thought the body was made to rule. However, the body only desires things of the world: lust of the flesh, lust of the eye, the pride of life. These are not of the Father.

Evaluate your personal life. Who's in control? Who's guiding your every move? To do great works, reverse the order. Place the spirit back in it's rightful place as king. As a born-again believer, God gave you dominion in your spirit over the soul and body. When asked the question, "Do you have dominion?" Be ready to reply, "Yes". But carry it out to the fullest by looking like you have dominion. Your appearance must not be sad, depressed, or defeated. Talk like it. Your speech reveals either dominion or defeat. Walk like it. Keep your shoulders high and walk with victory in every step. Dominate the life you live by living your life through the spirit.

 # Devotion 19:
# Victorious

*"When you pass through the waters, I will be with you;
and through the rivers, they shall not overflow you. When
you walk through the fire, you shall not be burned, nor
shall the flame scorch you."*

Isaiah 43:2


To the glory of God we are blessed. There are no ifs, ands, or buts about it. You and I are blessed. When we look back over our lives oh my, we see hills and valleys we've come over. We can see storms and rains we've come through. Yet, not one casualty is evident. We won in spite of the opposition. We stood despite the blows; we've recovered! Mercy and grace kept us. Faith brought us through. Love surrounded us. Peace made us. Thanks be to God who has caused us to triumph. To the glory of God Amen. Amen! We are victorious! Thanks be unto God who always causes us to triumph! Put a smile on your face and rejoice! Amen!

Other Verses: Isaiah 43:3-7

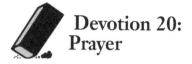

# Devotion 20:
# Prayer

*"Thus says the Lord who made it, the Lord who formed it to establish it (the Lord is His name): 'Call to Me, and I will answer you, and show you great and mighty things, which you do not know.'"*

Jeremiah 33:2-3

I have a Bluetooth speaker and when it is turned on to connect to my phone, it gives the following message: "Bluetooth on. Pairing. Connected." Once the message finishes, the music from my phone is then heard through the speaker. When, however, the battery power runs down, the connection ends, and the speaker must be plugged into an electrical power source to be recharged. We have a Bluetooth connection at all times to our Father in Heaven that never loses its connection. This connection called prayer is a constant connection that we have access to no matter where we are, what we're doing, or who we're with, and can be used to access the full power source of God Almighty.

There's never a time we have to be without the dynamic sound of His Holy Spirit speaking to us. He speaks to us to grant us wisdom from on high, peace in chaotic situations, and strength in our weakest state of being. Prayer is our connection that only loses connection when we fail to utilize its full potential. By not spending time connected to the power source of our God and Father we fail to stay connected. Turn on your Bluetooth of Prayer and listen. You'll clearly be able to hear the sound of the Spirit as He speaks directly to you in a full theater-style surround sound with no interruptions or breaks in connections. Call upon the power source! He's near and awaiting to be paired to you.

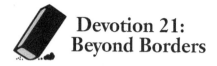

# Devotion 21:
# Beyond Borders

*"Enlarge the place of your tent, and let them stretch
out the curtains of your dwellings. Do not spare;
Lengthen your cords, and strengthen your stakes. For
you shall expand to the right and to the left, and your
descendants will inherit the nations, and make the
desolate cities inhabited."*

Isaiah 54:2-3

What's your first thought when you hear the word relationship? Do you think of a married couple or perhaps someone who's dating or even family ties? Relationships stretch far past family. Everyday whenever we go to work, to the grocer, doctor or for a walk, we cross paths of people whose lives we could enter into a relationship with. In our neighborhoods, there are opportunities for relationships to develop among neighbors. On our jobs, we can cultivate relationships of unity. At sporting events, we have the opportunity to establish interpersonal relationships. Even at the gas station, opportunity lies to create relationships.

For relationships to happen, we must be willing to extend beyond our borders of mistrust and take a leap of faith to show ourselves friendly. We must resist the standoff-ish behavior where we only allow people so far into our space and then insert a wall where they can go no further. Instead we need to exhibit behavior that is a result of time spent in God's presence and unconditional love. As we realize the Father's acceptance of us unconditionally, we too can give the world what it needs most, love without stipulations or boundaries. Stretch forth your hand; extend your reach; take off the limits of conditional; give love unconditionally. Everywhere you go healthy relationships can be planted and cultivated to grow and thrive.

# Devotion 22:
## Stand On Promise

*"Forever, O Lord, Your word is settled in heaven. Your faithfulness endures to all generations; You established the earth, and it abides."*

Psalm 119:89-90

If you know that you know that you know God said "it", then stand on it. Things may not appear as you believed they would, but stand adamantly on His promised word. He can't fail you. Heaven and earth may pass away but the Word of God shall last forever. Go ahead and grin and bear whatever is before you. This too shall pass and it's working for your good. God has spoken. Let the church say, "Amen!" Hallelujah! In the words of Mr. Rogers, from the PBS children's series, Mr. Rogers Neighborhood, "It's a beautiful day in the neighborhood!"

Other Verses: Psalm 119:91-96

# Devotion 23:
# Miracle Time

*"And they went out and preached everywhere, the Lord working with them and confirming the word through the accompanying signs."*

Mark 16:20

When the time is right for a miracle, nothing can stop what needs to happen! It's miracle time and it is in your hands to make it happen. It's in your mouth to speak it forth. It's in your feet to walk right into the miraculous. The time is right! The time is now! The one catch to this is the miracle isn't for you, it for the person or persons you'll encounter today.

So, get up and get ready to release the blessing of a miracle into the life of someone who stands in need of a miraculous move in their life. Miracles, signs, and wonders follow those who believe! To the glory of God set the atmosphere for release. Praise God! Speak life! Release faith! Expect the miraculous! God is able to do through you exceedingly, abundantly, more than you can ask or think today. Hallelujah! This is our day for the miraculous!

# Devotion 24:
# Revival

*"Will You not revive us again, that Your people may*
*rejoice in You? Show us Your mercy, Lord, and grant us*
*Your salvation."*

Psalm 85:6-7

Hallelujah! Thine the glory! Hallelujah! Amen! Hallelujah! Thine the glory! Revive us again! He's doing it now even as we speak, sing or think those thoughts. Revival has begun in your life and mine. The devil tried to make us think we were at the end of the rope but "No sir. It's not over until we win!" None of us enter the day with losing on our mind and neither does our Father. In fact, we are victorious because of Christ Jesus.

The revival of our hopes, dreams, and desires are all within plain sight. Grab what's yours. Nothing can come between what God has promised and what we're willing to receive. Praise God for this day of revival. Next year this time we'll be saying to everyone who'll listen, "Do you remember that day? It was a great day of revival in my life. Let me tell you about it!"

 **Devotion 25:
Rest**

*"Come to Me, all you who labor and are heavy laden,
and I will give you rest. Take My yoke upon you and learn
from Me, for I am gentle and lowly in heart and you will
find rest for your souls."*

Matthew 11:28-29

A re you tired physically, emotionally, and even mentally? Rest from your labor. Many people in America celebrate Labor Day each year with a day off from their jobs. While some aren't afforded this day off, countless others will spend time relaxing with family and friends while ending the last of summer vacations. Often, little is actually done that can be called rest but it is time away from the bump and grind of a day at work. Rest in the natural requires you to slow down, relax, and put your mind on something other that the daily routine found in our overactive lives.

Rest in the spirit is similar. Here we must slow down, cast our cares on the God who never slumbers nor sleeps, and trust in Him. To rest we need to trust that He will carry us daily whether at home, on our jobs, in the hospital, or wherever we may find ourselves. Even in the midst of hurricanes and tropical storms of life, He gives rest. Resting in God's care is inevitably the best rest one can find. Come unto Him if you're heavy laden and you'll find rest. You'll find strength like no other in Him. Call upon Him today. He's near and He shall surely give you rest.

 **Devotion 26:**
**Refuge**

*"He has redeemed my soul in peace from the battle that was against me, for there were many against me."*

Psalm 55:18

Where can you go for refuge of your soul? Nowhere but to the Lord. He'll renew your mind. He'll calm your emotions. He'll challenge your intellect. He'll conform your will to His. He'll change the canvas of your imagination to a picture of your future in Him. If you go to Him in prayer, refuge can be found. Sanctity and resolute peace are in His presence. Where could I go? Where could I go? Seeking a refuge for my soul. Where could I go but to the Lord, but to the Lord! Praise God.

 # Devotion 27:
# Serving

*"Give, and it will be given to you: good measure, pressed down, shaken together, and running over will be put into your bosom. For with the same measure that you use, it will be measured back to you."*

Luke 6:38

When the call to serve comes at you, during a time you feel you're already giving your all, answer it! There's something awaiting you that will pull together all the missing pieces and place you at a vantage point over your enemies. Yes. Service conquers the enemy of your soul. Service causes you to focus on others rather than your needs or shortcomings.

To serve is to give. To give opens a window where you'll be able to receive the bountiful blessings awaiting release. The act of serving others releases the blessing that is a residual blessing. Like the Energizer Bunny, the blessing keeps going and going and going. The blessing is a constant flow to meet your needs and enable you to supersede even your own expectations. Find a place to serve today and watch what happens. The blessing shall flow. Give and it shall be given unto you. What is the "it"? It's the reward that comes with having a heart to serve and the life of being an ideal servant.

# Devotion 28:
# New Life

*"Come now, and let us reason together," Says the
Lord, "Though your sins are like scarlet, they shall be
as white as snow; Though they are red like crimson,
they shall be as wool."*

Isaiah 1:18

The ways of man are such that God knows them all. So He searches the heart to know the motives. Nothing is hidden. Nothing left covered before His all seeing eyes. He sees and He knows. Be not dismayed. He cares for you even as He searches the darkest crevice of a heart ridden with hurt, pain, disappointment, and disgust. He cleanses it through the washing of the blood of Jesus. A blackened heart dipped in the warmth of His precious red blood produces a clean, vibrant heart that awakens the soul to new life found in Christ Jesus. A new citizenship is issued and a new way of life begins. What can wash away our sin? Nothing but the blood of Jesus!

 **Devotion 29:
He Answers**

*"The righteous cry out, and the Lord hears, and delivers
them out of all their troubles."*

Psalm 34:17

When you believe you've searched and searched and there's no other place to look, look to the hills. Your help is in the Lord. When you feel you've called out and no one hears, cry out to God. God is attentive to your cry. When you feel you've knocked at every door possible, knock one more time. Knock and the door shall be opened. The problem is not what you've been doing to seek relief. The problem is in what or whom you've sought relief. Jesus is the answer. However, most often He's not our first option. Nevertheless, He stands with open arms to receive us. Cry out to Jesus. He'll open doors, answer prayers, and come down to see about His blood-bought brother and sister. He's the answer for the world today. Above him there's no other. Jesus is the way. Amen.

Other Verses: Psalm 34:1-22

 **Devotion 30: Release**

*"Therefore if the Son makes you free, you shall be free indeed."*

John 8:36

Laying to rest all the hurt of the past is a desire we all have at some point in time. It's easier said than done. However, as you bear in mind the grace of a Father, as you recall the warmth of His presence, and as you stand on the foundation of His word, a new sound that touches Heaven emits from deep within. Our reservations and even misconceptions are replaced with the peace found in the release.

Release every concern to God and expect Him to do what He's promised concerning your situation. He alone is God and well able to do what's needed for you in this hour and every hour from henceforth! Praise His holy and wondrous name! Release the hurt. Release the pain. Release the offense. Release God to release you from the things, and even the people, who have had you bound. Freedom is imminent as you release. Verbally release as you inwardly praise the Father for this new found freedom. Liberty comes in the spoken release. Receive liberty and move into destiny! Amen.

 **Devotion 31:
Chosen**

*"You did not choose Me, but I chose you and appointed
you that you should go and bear fruit, and that your fruit
should remain, that whatever you ask the Father in My
name He may give you."*

John 15:16

Around 1992, New Horizon Church and Its
Ministries, Inc. recorded an album. One of the
songs we sang was entitled, "He Chose Me."
Out of all the people He could use, God chose me?
Wow! What a show of confidence on His part. I mean,
with all that I believe I'm not, He looked beyond my
faults and still chose me. Oh my! Heaven sees my best
so I must refuse to see anything less. He chose me. The
summons can not be overlooked by me. He chose me.
I'm His workmanship. I'm His representative. I'm His.
Hence, I rejoice in the fact that out of all the people He
could use, He chose me.

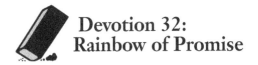

# Devotion 32:
# Rainbow of Promise

*"Nevertheless I will remember My covenant with you in the days of your youth, and I will establish an everlasting covenant with you."*

Ezekiel 16:60

One day as I drove home from the airport, I looked to my left and in the sky was a rainbow. There was no rain, but in the eastern sky, I could see the faint colors of the rainbow. The story of Noah and the promised covenant came to mind. Then as I looked again, to my amazement once more, a second rainbow was just above the first. I believe God was confirming His covenant to me once again.

The Lord has not been slack toward His promises to me in any shape, form, or fashion. If anything, it has been me who has failed to stand upon His covenant promises. So on my part I repent and turn back to the author and finisher of my faith. Although the appearance of the rainbow served as a reminder to me, God's word is an ever present covenant. I can use it daily to confirm and manifest the covenant promises He's made to me. You can do the same. He's faithful to fulfill His promises. Let's be faithful to receive every one whether they come in bulk or one promise at a time. As He keeps His word, we too shall know that He is God, the covenant keeper! To God be the Glory for the covenant He has given us!

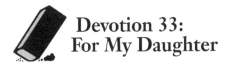

# Devotion 33:
# For My Daughter

*"Charm is deceitful and beauty is passing, But a woman who fears the Lord, she shall be praised."*

Proverbs 31:30

As the days turned to hours and knowing very shortly the hours shall be minutes, I looked over at the sleeping princess who had been home a little over a month. My daughter was now preparing to leave again for yet another year of college and a second degree, I knew I would miss her so much! She's been such a joy to have home and a workhorse assisting me with everything I've done since her arrival. As I glance at her and hear the soft breaths as she does her usual task of sleeping while I drive, tears are welling up in my eyes. I'm blessed to have her as my daughter.

I know that someday soon there is a man who shall be blessed to have her as his wife. I know her daddy's smiling, with his chest poked out in joy because of the progress all four of his children have made. She, however, was his baby and I know her name rings loudly in Heaven's gates. I love you Arielle. I anxiously anticipated Christmas break that year and her arrival home again. Keep on the track of the Proverbs 31 woman. You're on target!

 **Devotion 34: Mercy**

*"This I recall to my mind, Therefore I have hope. Through the Lord's mercies we are not consumed, because His compassions fail not. They are new every morning; Great is Your faithfulness."*

Lamentations 3:21-23

This I call to mind. Therefore, I have hope. It is because of the Lord's mercies we are not consumed. By His mercy we are not consumed by the snares of the enemy, the assaults of our foes, or the consequences of our mistakes. God's mercies are fresh and anew every morning. His mercy endures forever. When we call upon Him, He answers. Nothing ever catches Him by surprise for He's all knowing. There's no place we can go from His presence for He's everywhere.

No power is greater than His authority or dominion for He is all powerful. The reign of the governments will be upon His shoulders. It doesn't matter the current state of the nation, when America returns to its first love He shall answer every prayer. If we, the people who are called by His name and are called according to His purpose, will humble ourselves in prayer, seek His face instead of His hand, turn from the wickedness of our hearts, He'll hear our prayer. He'll forgive the errors we've made because of a sin-conscious mind rather than the renewed mind of Christ Jesus. He'll heal the chaos. He'll erase the struggle. He'll provide the calming balm of Gilead to cleanse us of all unrighteousness. Yes indeed!

When we turn back to Him, He shall restore us back into the position as sons and kingdom authority. Tell yourself, "I'm a child of the King!" Be an imitator of the King! Reign in authority by the creative words you speak and the royal priesthood actions you make. Jesus is Lord! We reign in authority with Him. It's time to seek Him as never before. For His return is imminent. We cannot afford to let Him catch us with our work incomplete. So let's work while it is day; giving our best effort unto the Master! Speak the word of God and cancel all negativity. Hallelujah! Thine the glory! Hallelujah! Amen! Hallelujah! Thine the glory! Revive us again!

Other Verses: 2 Chronicles 7:13-14

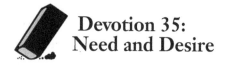 ## Devotion 35:
## Need and Desire

*"Seek the Lord while He may be found, Call upon Him while He is near."*

Isaiah 55:6

I need thee. Oh I need thee. Every hour I need thee. Oh bless me now, my Savior. I come to thee. There were perhaps periods in our lives we didn't fully grasp the knowledge of just how much we really needed God. One day, however, it was apparent that we're nothing without him. Still as we grew and in the fullness of time our need became desire. Now we both want and need a substantive relationship where not only our needs are met but we live lives that are well-pleasing to Him.

He's our anchor and the solid rock on which we stand. He's more than enough and well-able to pull us from the flames of sin and sting of death. In return, every day we remind Him of our need. With our desire we seek Him earnestly through the daily actions of our lives. When need becomes desire our lives change. To the glory of God, Father, we need you!

# Devotion 36:
## All Is Well

*"...And she said, "It is well."*

2 Kings 4:23

All is well! No matter what it looks like. No matter the pain you are in. No matter the hurt you have suffered. No matter what, "All is well!" So you say, " but you don't know what I'm going through." Truth is, I don't. However, I know who's going through with you and the truth is, He shall bring you through. Don't faint. Your breakthrough comes as you go through. Proudly proclaim, "All is well!" Read 2 Kings 4. Just as He did for this person, so shall He do for you! All is well and yes, that's my final answer!

# Devotion 37:
# Keep Running

*"But those who wait on the Lord shall renew their strength; They shall mount up with wings like eagles, they shall run and not be weary, they shall walk and not faint."*

Isaiah 40:31

Just because you've been released from limitations doesn't mean the enemy won't throw roadblocks in front of you. When this happens be like the mustard seed and maneuver around the barrier. The enemy's job is to stop your progress. This however, shall not be. Even if you run smack dab into the barrier, regroup, shake yourself and proceed around. A detour only opens your eyes to what you haven't seen before. Scan the area and run in. Destiny awaits your continued progress. The King has opened the gates before you and awaits your arrival. Your mission shall be accomplished on time!

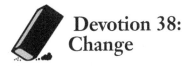 **Devotion 38: Change**

*"The Spirit of the Lord shall rest upon Him, The Spirit of wisdom and understanding, The Spirit of counsel and might, The Spirit of knowledge and of the fear of the Lord."*

Isaiah 11:2

As a teacher, each year I return to work after a brief but professional development packed "summer break." Things may not be perfect but we always adapt. In the terms of the old Program for Effective Teaching or P.E.T. Model, (Yes, I am just that old), we'll task analyze the situation, monitor and adjust, as needed. Nevertheless, as the final hours of our summer vacation draw to a close Isaiah 11:2-5 are always a prayer for me. I meditate on these scriptures daily. It's really my confession that I wish to share with you.

I decree this over your lives. "The Spirit of the Lord will alight and rest upon you. By the Spirit of wisdom and discernment, you will shine like the dew. By the Spirit of counsel and strength, you will judge fairly and act courageously. By the Spirit of knowledge and reverence of the Lord. You will take pleasure in honoring the Lord. You will determine fairness and equity; You will consider more than what meets the eye and weigh in more than what you're told. So that even those who can't afford a good defense will nevertheless get a fair and equitable judgment. With just a word, you will end wickedness and abolish oppression. With nothing more than the breath of your mouth, you will destroy evil. You will clothe yourself with righteousness and truth; the impulse to right wrongs will be in your blood." As these words are spoken and manifested over your lives be blessed today, henceforth, now and forevermore. Amen!

Tell yourself: Seasons change. Relationships change. People change. Change is destined to happen. Questions change. Responses change. Lives change. Change is often met with resistance. The change I want to see inevitably starts with me. I am a catalyst both for and of change. Each day opportunity for change exists that will develop me into the image of God's Son. I seize the opportunity knowing that of all that's changing around me, Jesus Christ is the same yesterday, today, and forevermore. I am fixed on this one thing, to be like Him.

Other Verses: Isaiah 11:1-5, Hebrews 13:8

 # Devotion 39:
# Mustard Seed Faith

*"So Jesus said to them, "Because of your unbelief; for assuredly, I say to you, if you have faith as a mustard seed, you will say to this mountain, 'Move from here to there,' and it will move; and nothing will be impossible for you."*

Matthew 17:20

If you have faith the size of a mustard seed, you can do anything. The potential is in you to be greater than anyone in your ancestry lineage. However, to activate the potential you must first believe it to be so. Next, you must demonstrate your belief by speaking words that bring life to the potential. Then, you must initiate corresponding actions that demonstrate your faith.

Is your faith in what God has said or rather in what people or circumstances have made you to believe? That mustard seed faith to move mountains is in you. It's up to you to activate it. Since faith comes by hearing, you need to listen to yourself adamantly decree the blessings of the Abrahamic Covenant over your life. Declare it over your possessions, children and loved ones. Make it your lot today to let your faith move for you. Mustard seed faith! That's all you need.

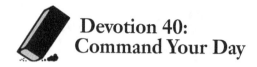

# Devotion 40:
# Command Your Day

*"As it is written, "I have made you a father of many nations," in the presence of Him whom he believed - God, who gives life to the dead and calls those things which do not exist as though they did."*

Romans 4:17

What's happening in your life that makes you smile? Think about it. What goes on in your sphere that causes you to look forward to each new day? Run to it. What words are heard that give you hope for tomorrow? Listen for them. Each day we could dwell on the pain, focus on the struggle, or even wallow in sorrow but each day there's good all around us. There's greatness in our midst. There's the potential to excel. The best of the best days of our lives are dependent upon the attitude we take. Whatever we set our focus on will determine our day.

The thing you contemplate the most shall surely come to pass. Think on the things that bring peace as you call circumstances that aren't as though they were. Think and speak out of your mouth what you desire for each day. Command your day by the words you say. Grace, prosperity, favor, increase, success, influence, and peace are mine today. I said it and I'm not changing it. What will you say for yourself? Say it loud and clear. Command your day!

 **Devotion 41:**
**With A Smile**

*"I can do all things through Christ who strengthens me."*

Philippians 4:13

As I drive into the city, I daily pass a man who is wheelchair bound. He is always sitting near the edge of his driveway. As each car passes, he throws up a hand and with the biggest smile waves and nods hello. He's always smiling and can be found at the same location at least twice a day, greeting all who come by. His driveway is rocky so I know it takes great effort to make his way to his daily perch. Despite the barriers that seemingly could exist, he is faithful to be in place every day. Whatever the obstacle you may face, face it with a smile. Face it head on. You too can overcome and smile as the man I described above. You can do all things because greater is He that lives in you than any barrier you may face. Grace and peace be multiplied to you today!

# Devotion 42:
# Shine

*"Let your light so shine before men, that they may see your good works and glorify your Father in heaven."*

Matthew 5:16

You don't have to be a star to be in God's show. He's looking for raw talent that He can develop. The cost to shine is relatively inexpensive. It requires the release of your life to Him but if you're selling yourself out to someone anyway, why not to the King of Glory? The benefits on the other hand are well worth the sacrifice and receipt of the ultimate reward is non-negotiable. The price for your stardom has been paid so there are no hidden costs.

The only lines you must read between are those that separate you into holiness, righteousness, sanctification, and justification. All of which bring you back to the original covenant drawn up between God and Abraham. The covenant for your stardom cannot be altered. You're set to be a star. You may as well shine. You're a shining star, no matter who you are. Shine your light to see who you can truly be.

# Devotion 43:
# The Impossible

*"But Jesus looked at them and said to them, "With men this is impossible, but with God all things are possible."*

Matthew 19:26

He did it again! He made a way! He moved mountains of hurt, fear, disappointment and grief. He caused walls of heartache, vindictiveness, and malice to fall. He turned the impossibilities into realities and there is nothing that's impossible for Him, nor you. Guess what! He's done all this before the day has even begun. You don't even have to expect it, just know He cares for you and has already completed the process that you're walking through. Don't stop! Faith is before you. He knows what lies ahead. Go on with faith!

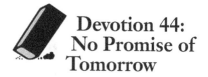

# Devotion 44:
# No Promise of
# Tomorrow

*"Whereas you do not know what will happen tomorrow. For what is your life? It is even a vapor that appears for a little time and then vanishes away."*

James 4:14

Some time ago, I was reflecting on just how much time I spend contemplating what I'm going to do tomorrow. Then in my heart I heard the lyrics to the song "Tomorrow," as sung by the Winans. In this version, a definitive statement is made which in its simplest terms says, "Tomorrow is not promised." In the reality of this statement, we can't change the past. Tomorrow isn't promised. So let's choose to live today as if there was no tomorrow. Let's get it right with loved ones we feud with and don't even remember why or how it started. Let's make it right with those who we have issues with that the root cause was something as trivial as someone walking by without speaking. Oh my, Lord!

Don't you realize there are hundreds, if not thousands of people, who'd give anything to have the opportunity to spend time with a departed loved one?

Yet here we sit, obstinate and adamant that "until he/she apologizes I am not saying anything to them." Well, you apologize. It doesn't matter who started it. It only matters how it ends.

In baseball, one pitcher may start the game, but if need be, the general manager will have him pulled to salvage a win. The pitcher who comes in for him receives credit for the save but the first pitcher didn't suffer a loss. Today is the day to decide, I'm not going to let any relationship suffer a loss. You're the saving pitcher and the game is in your hand. Don't put off until tomorrow, for tomorrow very well could be too late.

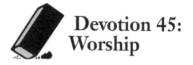

# Devotion 45: Worship

*"And the King will answer and say to them, 'Assuredly, I say to you, inasmuch as you did it to one of the least of these My brethren, you did it to Me.'"*

Matthew 25:40

I've got something to say. Not specifically to you, but instead to our Father in Heaven. Basically, I just want to tell Him the following words, "Here I am to worship. Here I am to bow down. Here I am to say, "You're my God!"" We each have words that we feel we must utter unto the Lord. As simple as they may be, when the words we speak correlate with the actions we do, there is great impetus for others to see the image of the true and living God.

We're not oblivious to the needs of our brothers and sisters. Nor do we neglect to render service as unto the Lord. Since we are His hands and feet upon the earth, let us feed God's sheep. Let us be ready to respond in the affirmative when questioned about our adherence to His commands of loving our brethren as ourselves. Worship is action packed and requires movement of some kind. God is honored by our service to our fellow man.

Think about the following small act of service that carries with it great reward. Commit to helping a family in the purchase of school supplies. A pack of pencils, crayons, glue sticks, erasers, hand sanitizer, loose leaf paper, spiral notebook and a composition notebook can be purchased at Walmart for less than $5.00. Donate this to a child. The child will remember, and the parent will have those extra dollars to spend elsewhere. You know, you could take it one step further and ask your church to collect and distribute these items to children in your congregation. Then you could present any leftover items to your neighborhood school. When a child comes without supplies, your act of worship provides an answered need. However you present worship today, do it as the gift of service to someone. Worship him today in service and not words alone. Let service be what's trending today on your timeline of life.

# Devotion 46:
# Do Not Worry

*"But seek first the kingdom of God and His righteousness,
and all these things shall be added to you."*

Matthew 6:33

Have you ever been up early enough to hear the birds just chirping away? The sounds they vocalize are not sounds of distress, worry or anxiety. Instead the sounds we hear are bright, cheerful and upbeat. In fact, they cause us to wonder, and even question, the basis for the joyful sound that's flowing from deep within them. Perhaps they realize the fact we have to be reminded of, God is good and His mercy endures forever.

He's so good to them, so much so, that the birds can only sing praises to Him for they know He constantly cares for their well-being. He adamantly stands to protect them. They are securely nestled in the safety of His arms. Their needs are met even before the day breaks. So they sing unto the Father who is El Shaddai, the all-sufficient one.

You know, you and I can sing with them for God cares for us even more so. After all, we're made in His image. We're called His sons and daughters. We are His authorized representatives on earth. Who's to say that only the birds have reason to sing? It isn't true. So, do we. "I sing because I'm happy. I sing because I'm free. His eyes are on the sparrow and I know He watches me."

Other Verses: Matthew 6:25-32

# Devotion 47:
# Into The Deep

*When He had stopped speaking, He said to Simon,*
*"Launch out into the deep and let down your nets*
*for a catch."*

Luke 5:4

A re you tired of doing the same thing in the same place, at the same time? Does it seem you've been here in this position forever with no change at all? Does it appear that although you're doing the right things, you are getting little to no results? If so, take this piece of wisdom, pull out into the deep and cast your net on the other side. Chances are, you're in too shallow of a place to get the desired results you're both seeking, and deserve.

The big catch is in the deep. However, where you are now, the best you'll ever catch is top water bream. True fishermen know that just because a favorite fishing hole produces a grand catch time after time, doesn't mean it will be this way forever. Eventually the hole will dry up. Either the fish move or they've all been caught. There's no need for you to continue angling in a fishing hole that is empty of the financial resources, emotional support, unconditional love, and spiritual leadership you are seeking.

It's time to cast your net on the other side. As you pull out into the deep and cast your net on the other side, just like Peter you won't be able to pull in the bountiful catch alone. There's too much awaiting you for you to remain where you are. Move on! Make that move. On the other side of the boat is the best catch of the day!

Other Verses: Luke 5:1-11

# Devotion 48:
# His Love

*"For God so loved the world that He gave His only begotten Son, that whoever believes in Him should not perish but have everlasting life."*

John 3:16

Have you ever told God why you love Him? I mean we so loosely throw the word "love" around but how often do we toss it in His direction? We're quick to say, "I love you" and even faster on the draw to respond, "I love you, too." Think about how we openly announce our feelings of love to a person who makes us feel giddy inside when our Father is the one who gives and sustains our lives. Without God's intervention I don't know of anyone who has that ability. So, today reflect back on your relationship with the Father and from deep within the hidden crevices of your inner man, you'll probably hear these words crying out to God, "This is why I love You because You love me."

# Devotion 49:
# He Hears Us

*"For the eyes of the Lord are on the righteous, and His ears are open to their prayers; But the face of the Lord is against those who do evil."*

1 Peter 3:12

I awakened one morning to the voice of the late Deacon Espen Butler delivering the words to the hymn that was sung during countless prayer services at Harmony Baptist Church. It went like this, "I love the Lord. He heard my cry and pitied every groan. Long as I live when trouble rise, I'll hasten to His throne."

When God takes pity on us, He doesn't feel sorry for our situation or the condition we're in. Instead, He takes action. You see at the Cross when our Lord and Savior, Christ Jesus made the final declaration of, "It is finished!", He wasn't playing. Every debt was paid. Every bill erased. Every sin eliminated. Every demonic assault and oppression annihilated. He ransomed you and me with His blood.

So, when we cry out to our Father, Heaven becomes alert and active to the man that He is so very mindful of. His arm is not slack unto us because His ears are attentive to our cries. So don't be surprised at how deliverance comes today. Receive the move of the hand of God through the vessel He sends to bring you out. If you'll hasten to His throne, He's going to take action. Then you can sing the next verse of the hymn with blessed assurance: "I love the Lord. He bowed His head and chase my griefs away." Glory Hallelujah!

Other Verses: Psalm 34:15, 2 Chronicles 7:15

# Devotion 50:
# For Our Good

*"And we know that all things work together for good to those who love God, to those who are the called according to His purpose."*

Romans 8:28

You've made the move and now you're wondering, "Was it the right thing to do?" It was. Doesn't matter how you feel inside or what people say or how they stare. You lived in faith. You obeyed God. You not only stepped across the finish line; you won the race. You didn't just end a chapter; you closed the book. It's time to start conditioning for the next marathon. It's time to write your next Pulitzer Prize-Winning Bestseller. Don't look back in heartache. Look ahead with joyful expectation. Release your friend and servant named faith to bring what you need to continue on life's journey. He's waiting. So be at peace for all things work together for your good even the move you just made.

# Devotion 51:
# Go Ahead

*"The one who breaks open will come up before them;*
*They will break out, pass through the gate, and go out*
*by it; Their king will pass before them, with the Lord*
*at their head."*

Micah 2:13

Make that move you've been pondering over. Go ahead. You're unsettled and there's a constant battle going on in your mind because you know "you gotta do what you gotta do." Time is of the essence. There's little time left and the timing is right. Go ahead. You've prayed. You've fasted. You've found scriptures to quote. You know it's the right time. So be like Nike and "Just Do It!" God has gone before you. The way is clear. Everything works for your good. Just Do It!

Other Verses: Romans 8:28

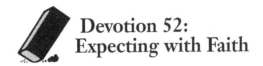# Devotion 52:
# Expecting with Faith

*"Now faith is the substance of things hoped for, the evidence of things not seen."*

Hebrews 11:1

Anticipation makes you wait but expectation allows you to see what you're anticipating as if it's already in your reach. Anticipation sparks the appetite but expectation allows you to taste what you are anticipating. Anticipation causes one to desire more and more of the substance longed for but expectation puts the desire in a position to receive. You see, anticipation comes with a fellow named "longing for" while expectation comes with a force called "faith". Faith goes out and gets what you're expecting while longing for sits backs and anticipates. Now you can wait around longing for with anticipation or you can put faith to work and bring what you're expecting to you. The choice is yours. As for me, I'm expecting with faith! Hallelujah, I see Him coming now with what I expected! Glory to God!

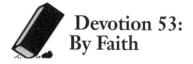 **Devotion 53:**
**By Faith**

*"For we through the Spirit eagerly wait for the hope of*
*righteousness by faith."*

Galatians 5:5

When you're put in the position to make a move you really didn't want to make in the first place, what do you do? Well there are options. One of which can only make matters worse. A second that can leave things basically as they are and eventually make matters worse. The third is to move ahead. All three options have life altering ramifications behind them. Yet, the first two options are based on fear and will literally stop you dead in your tracks or even cause you to retreat. The third option and often final is an act of faith.

By faith move ahead. By faith believe that all things work together for your good. Also know that this action works good in the lives of those you are associated with. We're in a season of unlimited possibilities. Yet, the options we choose will determine the lid, if any, we put on what's before us. I want to believe my possibilities are limitless. However, I must proceed with faith.

From this point on in my life, faith is my escort. Faith is my servant. Faith is the advance party that goes ahead to have everything I need in place when I arrive at my destinations (for there are many). He's here at your disposal too. Don't dispose of him. Utilize this invaluable asset. So, in looking at the options you have, look through the eyes of faith and you'll soon realize moving ahead should always be your first and final option.

Other Verses: Hebrews 11:1, 1 Peter 1:7, 1 John 5:4

 **Devotion 54:
How You Wait**

*"Therefore you also be ready, for the Son of Man is coming
at an hour you do not expect."*

Luke 12:40

What are you waiting for? A phone call or a text message? An email? A letter? What are you expecting? Blessings to overtake you? Multiple streams of income? Anointing of grace, mercy, peace? How are you waiting? In patience? Without murmuring or complaining? Joyfully? Giving thanks?

No matter what you are waiting for or expecting, the attitude in which you wait can impede or accelerate what is coming to you. Have you noticed that when you speak about your circumstances your "peeps" put on the same attitude you've taken? Hence, set an atmosphere to receive what you're expecting? You'll soon discover that what you are waiting for and expecting will get to you a lot sooner than you anticipated.

Other Verses: Psalm 123:2, Luke 12:35-40

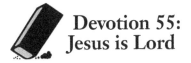 # Devotion 55:
## Jesus is Lord

*"For unto us a Child is born, unto us a Son is given;*
*And the government will be upon His shoulder. And His*
*name will be called Wonderful, Counselor, Mighty God,*
*Everlasting Father, Prince of Peace."*

Isaiah 9:6

To the One who sits upon the throne there is given glory, honor, and majesty. His reign is everlasting. His truth endures throughout generations. He is Lord. Jesus is Lord. He reigns supreme. He is captain over the angelic hosts. Even today to His kingdom there is no end.

Rejoice! Shout with a voice of triumph! The heavens declare His glory! The children of God sing forth His praise! To the glory of God we resound with great joy that He is King of kings and Lord of lords. Jesus Christ, the Messiah is our Savior divine, balm in Gilead, Wonderful Counselor, Prince of Peace, Lion of the tribe of Judah, Lamb of God who took away the sins of the world. He is the living word who became flesh and took upon His shoulders the government of this world. I reiterate. Jesus is Lord! Jesus is Lord! Jesus is Lord! Give Him glory! Amen!

 **Devotion 56: Favor**

*"'For I will look on you favorably and make you fruitful, multiply youand confirm My covenant with you."*

Leviticus 26:9

Today's morning message is, God's grace is sufficient to meet everything you will face today. Put worship in the place of worry and let faith overcome each fear. Belief erases unbelief. Praise turns potential into an answered promise. Today is a great day to be alive and an even greater day to be a child of God.

Let the light of God shine through you. This is your day for miracles, signs, and wonders. Be at peace as you make preparations to receive bountiful blessings billowing in from every direction. From the north, south, east, and west blessings shall overtake you. Today is your day to receive! Put a praise on it, and watch it come to pass. To God be the glory! Amen.

Other Verses: Leviticus 26:1-13

# Devotion 57:
# Authority

*"Beware lest anyone cheat you through philosophy and empty deceit, according to the tradition of men, according to the basic principles of the world, and not according to Christ. For in Him dwells all the fullness of the Godhead bodily; and you are complete in Him, who is the head of all principality and power."*

Colossians 2:8-10

Code Black! There is an intruder in our midst. Alert all the proper ones in authority so they can assume their assigned position. Hold up a minute. We are the proper ones in authority. We've been granted access, given the code to unlock the building and granted the highest-level security clearance. We are the ones who have jurisdictional command of a set sphere of influence that allows us to flow freely across the globe, all while eradicating the enemy from every hamlet, village, town, city, state, and nation. Although he comes as a roaring lion, he's only blowing smoke. We are the original descendants of the Lion of the tribe of Judah! We roar with the kingdom authority of righteousness. Our ancestry dictates that we have victory over him.

Gird yourself up for war remembering that the weapons of our warfare are not carnal because the enemy we war against is not carnal. Instead, we fight in the spirit at all times. We fight knowing that our weaponry is mighty through God to the pulling down of all the enemy's strongholds. We release faith to go before us and get everything we need in this battle. As faith maneuvers through the spirit to obtain what's rightly ours, in earnest expectation we wait in the company of patience and praise. Peace joins us and constantly reminds us that the battle is not ours but the Lord's. Code Green! All is well! The Lord Jesus won this war ages ago. So, let us shout now as the enemy is annihilated before our eyes. To God be the glory forever! Amen!

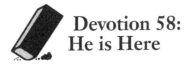

# Devotion 58:
# He is Here

*"Seek the Lord while He may be found, Call upon Him while He is near. Let the wicked forsake his way, and the unrighteous man his thoughts; Let him return to the Lord, and He will have mercy on him; And to our God, for He will abundantly pardon."*

Isaiah 55:6-7

I wasn't looking for Him. He found me. I didn't ask Him to hang around but He did so anyway. I didn't get His number, yet He answers whenever I call. He's here with me now. He's always near. His name is Jesus. His presence is ever so clear. So, should you call and I don't answer or come by and I don't come immediately to the door, it's probably because I'm talking to Him.

He's with you too. Listen and you'll hear Him. Be still and you'll feel him. He's here to give rest to the weary, bring peace to the chaos, relief to troubled minds, healing to the sick, strength to the weak, refreshing to the tired, joy to those in sorrow, and answers to all your questions. He's here for you and me both. Whatever we need He's here to provide. Ask and it shall be given. Seek and you'll find. Knock and He opens the door.

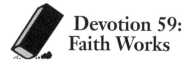

# Devotion 59:
# Faith Works

*"Then He arose and rebuked the wind and the raging of
the water. And they ceased, and there was a calm. But He
said to them, "Where is your faith?"*

Luke 8:24

This is only the beginning! What's begun in
your life shall surely be finished. You must
believe in the abilities you've been given. You
must adhere to the plan that has an expected end of
prosperity and success as its ultimate goal. You can't
give up nor give in. You're on the right track and in
the right lane. Stay the course. Run with patience and
diligence. Pace yourself. Exert extra energy only as
needed. You are designed to finish the race. You are
equipped to overcome every barrier that may come
before you.

Have faith in God's plan for you. Put faith to work
and allow Him to bring to you everything you need to
succeed. Here faith comes now. His only question for
you is? "What would you have me to do today?" Tell
Him. He's ready to bring it to pass. Faith is active and
ready to work for you.

I gotta go! I need to talk to my faith for a few minutes. I have a few things I need faith to do for me today! Well, what are you waiting for? You'd better put your faith to work too. Glory to God! The request is already in progress to be filled. Let Him do it for you. He merely has to pick it up and hand it to you. It's that simple. Let faith arise and work for you.

# Devotion 60:
# Fight Fear

*"Finally, brethren, whatever things are true, whatever things are noble, whatever things are just, whatever things are pure, whatever things are lovely, whatever things are of good report, if there is any virtue and if there is anything praiseworthy—meditate on these things."*

Philippians 4:8

Something happens when you're waiting on a call from a friend, a report from the doctor, test scores, results of a job interview and the list goes on. What usually happens is the enemy attacks on the battleground of the mind with fear and unbelief. What should not happen during the wait for a child of God is fear and unbelief.

Let me tell you how to counteract these two "hell derived emotions". First look up to Heaven and say, "I am a child of God Almighty!" Say it loud and distinctly. Don't stutter or hesitate. Next, lift your hands to heaven in submission to God's plan for this situation. Then, do a little dance of praise. Doesn't matter what it looks like to you. When God sees it, it looks like a great work of art or poetry in motion. Now, open your mouth again with praise. Rehearse in your heart scripture that embodies the word of truth you're standing on. Bless God for His mercy. Bless him for His faithfulness. Bless Him for His love that is everlasting. As you do these things you'll discover that even on the battleground of your mind you have victory! You win every time!

A good strategy to avoid unnecessary battles with fear and unbelief is to always think on the things that are true, just, lovely, pure and a good report. Doing this keeps you in a state of mind to crush the enemy in his tracks. Faith comes by hearing. So, as you rehearse what God says, faith in God becomes your trump card! Play Him as often as you need! You'll have the winning hand every time.

# Devotion 61:
# Faithful Guide

*"However, when He, the Spirit of truth, has come, He will guide you into all truth; for He will not speak on His own authority, but whatever He hears He will speak; and He will tell you things to come."*

John 16:13

One morning, a relatively dense fog had settled in. I was traveling down Highway 270 East between Pine Bluff and Malvern. Nevertheless, traffic was flowing at a normal speed, myself included. Occasionally, I came face to face with a pair of headlights. Then an oncoming vehicle quickly darted in front of the one he was passing to avoid our head-on collision! Despite the fog, traffic continued to flow.

There are times in life's journey when it appears we're in a dense fog. However, this is not the time to slow down, nor stop moving. We must continue to go with the flow. The flow of the Holy Spirit, that is. This unseen guide is equivalent to stealth radar. His accuracy in getting you safely from one point to the next is 100%. Trust Him to lead you through the denseness. He will safely guide you into a way where visibility is clear and you're free to accelerate to greater speeds. Oh yes, while you're in the fog, He will comfort you. No need to worry. He's got everything in His control. Soon you'll be as I am now, out of the fog and moving merrily right along.

# Devotion 62:
# Greater Love

*"Greater love has no one than this, than to lay
down one's life for his friends."*

John 15:13

One Fourth of July, my night ended literally with a bang. Throughout the neighborhood and town, fireworks were heard into the wee hours of the morning. In previous years, when Patrick, Ben, and Arielle were home, I never noticed it before, possibly because they were amongst those out shooting fireworks. It didn't bother me. I just laid in bed reminiscing of days gone by when the excitement was in my front yard too. It's easy to forget the things that cause you to smile or warm your heart. It's easy not to value those celebratory times until their gone.

Family time may be overlooked until one day you realize all the family has grown up, gone away, and started families of their own. That's why it's so important to redeem the time you have now with the ones you love most. That was the first year my family had not shared this holiday. Each of us had "our own lives" going on. I'm thankful for the times we've celebrated each other, so that everyday becomes a holiday, when we're all together. I'm sure you do the same. If you have the chance, kiss your baby who may be much taller than you now. Hug your son who's about to be 30 years old. Call your aunt who's dementia causes her to ask the same question over and over again. Stop by the nursing facility to see a family member or friend who can't come see you. Let's make the most of the time we have with the ones we love. In the process we'll find that no greater love has a man or woman than to lay down their life for their brothers or sisters.

Other Verses: John 15:9-17

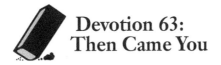

# Devotion 63:
# Then Came You

*"Love suffers long and is kind; love does not envy; love does not parade itself, is not puffed up; does not behave rudely, does not seek its own is not provoked, thinks no evil; does not rejoice in iniquity, but rejoices in the truth; bears all things, believes all things, hopes all things, endures all things. Love never fails."*

1 Corinthians 13:4-8

Remember Dionne Warwick and the song she sang? It said, "I never knew love before, then came you." We'd sing like we had someone very special. We really did and didn't even know it. For if we had known then like we know now of just how much God loves us nothing or no one else would even matter. We'd only have eyes for Him. We'd see our lives as being much stronger and better than what we do now. We'd even try harder to keep working our way back to Him.

Our love between God and us would stand as tall as the trees. Our love would be as deep as the seas. We'd know that come hell or high water, we are family. So no matter what we've done or said, we can sit ourselves down and talk to Him. We can tell Him what's on our mind. He merely responds, "Let's straighten it out". Through the Word of God, blood of Jesus, and guidance of the Holy Spirit, all things will work for our good. God's plans for us are intentional and never failing. So, as we keep love on our mind, this joy that we have cannot be taken from us. The world didn't give it and the world can't take it away. Like I said earlier, we never knew love before then came You, Lord. Then came you! Your love never fails. It never gives up on us!

 **Devotion 64:**
**Everlasting Love**

*"For God so loved the world that He gave His only*
*begotten Son, that whoever believes in Him should not*
*perish but have everlasting life."*

John 3:16

This will be an everlasting love and it's freely given to any and everyone who will receive! It's patient and kind. Its actions correspond to its words. It completed every task it's assigned with diligence and excellence. It's not self-serving neither is it boastful or full of arrogance or pride. This love endures. This love remains constant and steadfast. This love stays through storm and rain, sickness and pain. It's such a love that He died for us. As I said earlier, it's everlasting. Read John 3:16. Meditate on each phrase and you'll find that love was given with only one requirement, we must believe. Do you believe? So do I. Henceforth, now, and forevermore, this will be an everlasting love for me!

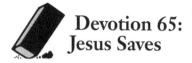 **Devotion 65:
Jesus Saves**

*"Therefore He is also able to save to the uttermost those
who come to God through Him, since He always lives to
make intercession for them."*

Hebrews 7:25

When I was a child, we sang a song and the words said, "To the utmost, Jesus saves." There's nothing too big He hasn't pulled us through. There's no distance He hasn't already covered. He's rescued us, time and time again, because to the utmost He saves.

The other car that backed into your lane and was a near miss, Jesus saved. The 18- wheeler that was going to force into the lane when there wasn't room, Jesus saved. The skillet left on the stove, which you thought about 30 minutes later, and came home to see smoke billowing from the roof. However, when you went inside, you only found smoke and no fire, Jesus saved.

Jesus not only opens doors to pull you through. He also closes doors to keep you from harm. To the utmost, Jesus saves. He will pick you up, turn you around, place your feet on solid ground. Jesus saves, Jesus saves.

Other Verses: Romans 8:38-39

# Devotion 66:
# A New Song

*"I will greatly rejoice in the Lord, My soul shall be joyful in my God; For He has clothed me with the garments of salvation, He has covered me with the robe of righteousness, as a bridegroom decks himself with ornaments, and as a bride adorns herself with her jewels."*

Isaiah 61:10

"I'm so excited and I just can't hide it! I'm about to lose control and I think I like it!" The Pointer Sisters sang these words when I was a teenager. We'd be dancing, jumping and yelling at the top of our lungs trying to sing along with them. Well today, I'm singing a new song with a different lead but the excitement is still there! The song I sing is because I'm happy. The song I sing is because I'm free. God's eyes are on the sparrow and I know He watches me.

God is opening doors of purpose for me. He's allowing fresh oil to be poured over me. I'm basking in His glory. I'm resting in His arms. For these reasons I'm so excited and I just can't hide it! I'm about to lose control and think I like it! Think about what He's done in your life and you too will find yourself singing, praising and worshipping! The garment of praise will be put on for the spirit of heaviness! That's a fact! Amen! Aren't you excited?

# Devotion 67:
# Self-Reflection

*"Thus says the Lord of hosts: "Consider your ways!"*

Haggai 1:7

Let us evaluate our lives each day we have breath. Did we do our best at whatever we did? Did we open our mouths to speak truth and favor to others? Was mercy at the forefront of our reactions? Was love present to make right the wrong we suffered or caused? Were we willing to forgive others? Were we careful to both hear and see with our hearts? Did we allow righteousness to prevail?

Not a day should pass that self-reflection through the magnifying lens of God's Word doesn't take place in our hearts. We are who we are and shall become more like Him because of His goodness, grace and mercy. When we self-evaluate and reflect on our actions, we enable God to continually finish the work He's begun in us. Self-reflection helps us to not get ahead of His plans for us. Maybe we should put forth more effort and move ahead, or maybe we should wait as patience possesses our souls. Whichever the case may be, as we self-evaluate we will more readily say, "not my will but Thy will be done." To the Glory of God Amen!

Other Verses: Jeremiah 29:11, Luke 21:19, Philippians 1:6

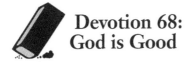 # Devotion 68:
# God is Good

*"Through the tender mercy of our God, with which the Dayspring from on high has visited us; To give light to those who sit in darkness and the shadow of death, to guide our feet into the way of peace."*

Luke 1:78-79

Even as the camera catches the dawn of this new day, our hearts can rejoice. For what's captured on film or digital imagery does not compare to the splendor of greatness that beckons us into this new day. Oh taste and see today that God's glory floods our environment. No evil can stay. Demonic assaults must cease. Angelic power is present and awaiting the sound of our voices to be released.

Righteousness, peace, and joy are before us as God's kingdom comes to earth as it is in Heaven. The Lord is good! Hallelujah! His mercy endures forever! His grace goes before us! Look! Our day awaits! Let's go get it with all diligence. As we earnestly expect to receive on today, it shall be so! Amen.

 **Devotion 69:
Opportunity**

*"Just as the Son of Man did not come to be served, but to
serve, and to give His life a ransom for many."*

Matthew 20:28

Going! Going! Gone! So goes every opportunity
we are given to be a light in the darkness.
When opportunity knocks we must answer
with certainty, knowing grace is given for us to answer
the call to serve. Are we willing? If so, let's get busy.
If not, the opportunity may not present itself again.
Each day make a concerted effort to move forward
in anticipation of making this day a day of service to
someone else.

Whether male or female, young or old, someone
is awaiting us to take advantage of the opportunity
we've been given. Jesus stands at the door and knocks,
providing opportunity for us to serve others as He did.
What would Jesus do? He'd siege every opportunity
and revolutionize the mindset of everyone He came in
touch with. As He is, so are we. Knock, knock. Who's
there? Opportunity. Opportunity who? Opportunity
for us to do as Jesus did and serve!

Other Verses: Mark 10:45, 1 John 4:17

# Devotion 70:
# Legacy

*"Therefore we also, since we are surrounded by so great
a cloud of witnesses, let us lay aside every weight, and
the sin which so easily ensnares us, and let us run with
endurance the race that is set before us, looking unto Jesus,
the author and finisher of our faith, who for the joy that
was set before Him endured the cross, despising the shame,
and has sat down at the right hand of the throne of God."*

Hebrews 12:1-2

As I look at the Planter's Peanut Man Meme leaping up in the air with the words "Way to GO!" in the background, I can't help but smile. It makes me think how happy our heavenly loved ones must be as they stand among the great cloud of witnesses, cheering us on in every effort we make to reach our goals.

I'm named after my adopted mother who is actually my great great aunt. She and "Deddy" made great sacrifices for my sister and me as we grew up in the rural community of Pine Grove five miles southeast of Sparkman. The last degree I received I wanted it to reflect a piece of them both so I included my maiden name of Brim. The degree came in the mail this week. The first night I held it and cried as I remembered how the Giles girls were my after-school tutors when

I needed additional help. Momma and Deddy always made provision when they were unable to meet our educational needs. That night I held the degree and smiled. I saw Momma and Deddy smiling too as they saw their name written on the fabric of the then six-year old they adopted in the summer of 1966. My smile grew as I saw the Lord standing behind them, He too smiled. It was then I realized that the words "Well done, thy good and faithful servant" could most certainly be heard by Momma and Deddy. The Lord thanked them for leaving a legacy for Theresa and me to emulate.

You know what we do on earth should be such that Heaven smiles when our names are mentioned on earth. Heaven is cheering us on in the background. We must keep the legacy of Christ going. Don't stop believing in yourself and your abilities. The past has shaped you for today but the future is awaiting you tomorrow. There's still time and opportunity. Go for the gusto in life! Leave a mark wherever you go that echoes the lives of those who touched your life and can be emulated by the ones whose lives you touch. One day, you too, will be amongst the great cloud of witnesses smiling and cheering on the legacy you've left behind.

 # Devotion 71:
## The Truth

*"And you shall know the truth, and the truth shall
make you free."*

John 8:32

We've once did a study at church that focused on building healthy relationships. The study had key concepts as to what's needed to build and sustain lasting relationships. Relationships that are healthy and not toxic. The study covers a plethora of relationships including marital, dating, business, friendship, male, female, and so on.

One morning I was awakened with the following thought, echoing in my spirit: "We can't build healthy relationships with anyone else until we first have a healthy relationship with ourselves." It starts in our personal time with the Lord, as we throw ourselves at the feet of the Father, and expose ourselves to the penetrating word of truth found in His word. Time spent in personal prayer and meditation on God's word, along with fellowship with other Christians and hearing the preached word, demands a root cause analysis of who we are and why we do what we do. Here we'll find out the truth behind why our relationships are as they are.

Guess what? The root cause has little to nothing to do with anyone else. It has to do with the "me" part of us in every relationship. As we continued the study and I was perhaps rolling my eyes, shooting unseen darts at the messengers for tapping into a place I've not wished to be tapped into. Would someone please let them know, "It's nothing personal against them. It's business. The business side of allowing God to make and mold me into the image of His dear Son as I'm set free from the bondage of the enemy within the inner me."

 **Devotion 72:**
**Great Grace**

*"But to each one of us grace was given according to
the measure of Christ's gift."*

Ephesians 4:7

Great grace! Great grace! Great grace! Great grace has been offered to us! Will we receive it? Grace stands taller than the highest mountain. Grace is heavier than the weightiest metal. It's more alive than life itself. It's more active than any molecule scientists have seen. Grace lives. Grace abounds. Grace awaits us wherever we must go. The power of grace is limitless. It's strength and value cannot be measured. Receive the grace needed for any and every situation. Great grace belongs to you. Expect it! Receive it! Apply it! "Grace, grace, God's grace, His grace is sufficient for me."

Other Verses: Acts 4:33

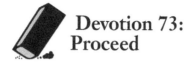

# Devotion 73:
# Proceed

*"The one who breaks open will come up before them; They will break out, pass through the gate, and go out by it; Their king will pass before them, with the Lord at their head."*

Micah 2:13

As I make my way down Hwy 270 East, clouds hang low amid the distant mountain peaks and a gentle, steady rain showers the road. Driving slightly below the speed limit, other motorists speed pass time on their way to various destinations unbeknownst to me.

Time is of the essence to arrive at our destinations at the appointed time. Traveling at our own pace, we each proceed cautiously. I pull over to pick up a bite to eat. I'm not going to sit and eat so the drive-thru is just fine. Placed my order, chatted with Candace, now back on the road again. The clouds are breaking. The rain has slacked up. Traffic is steady. Today's a great day! No detours! No sudden lane changes! Perfect traveling weather, as I journey on to my predestined destination.

So goes life. Rain comes. Clouds hang low. The mountain top seems in the far distance. People come into your life. People exit your life. Some move ahead.

Others stay behind. You may have to stop a few minutes to refuel your system. Yet, through life the final destination requires you to keep moving. Set a pace in God's Word and proceed. The road ahead is open for you to travel. Narrow is the way and not travelled by many, but the King has gone before you to open the gates and made the way clear for your travel. Move on, as you hear Him say, "You may proceed."

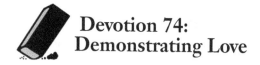

# Devotion 74:
# Demonstrating Love

*"The Lord has appeared of old to me, saying: "Yes, I have loved you with an everlasting love; Therefore with lovingkindness I have drawn you."*

Jeremiah 31:3

One evening, I went to a former student's house to say goodbye. He was moving to another city with his mom. Spending the past nine months with a person gives one a sense of belonging. To be quite honest, I looked upon him as my son. Despite our cultural, age, racial and other obvious differences, through our inward witness and outward expression of our love for Christ. We developed a common bond of love and mutual respect that transcended our differences and even translated into the lives of both our families.

There was a time when teachers were able to correct, chastise, console, and encourage without fear. In fact, teachers were considered the Latin term "in loco parentis". In modern terminology, "in the place of parents". I know my teachers assumed the role of Momma and Daddy. To be honest, the cafeteria workers, custodians and most definitely, the bus drivers all had been given the unspoken authority to make sure that we didn't "show out." So, since we knew this, we gave them the same respect that was given to our parents. They respected us and our parents while not abusing the silent authority they'd been given. Were schools better then? That's an individual answer we must give. However, I think I turned out alright. Your opinion may differ.

God's desire for us is to walk in His nature of love. As we do, we take His place on earth to demonstrate true unadulterated love that is given unconditionally. Goodbyes are always hard for me. Yet because of the connection between our families, a lifetime friendship among his family and mine had been established. God's love crosses physical, racial, cultural, and geographical boundaries. As our Lord loves us with an everlasting love we are to exemplify the same to everyone we meet. He's glorified as we do so. I pray the best for this former student, as I have done for every life I've been entrusted, as not just an educator, but as a representative of the Lord most high. So I pray, God be glorified through each of us as we represent Him on our jobs, in our homes, and in society as a whole. Let us always reflect the love God continually gives to each of us daily. Open opportunities, Lord for us to show others You through our actions and deeds. In Jesus name, Amen.

 **Devotion 75:
All Is Well**

*"Now it came to pass, when the vessels were full, that she
said to her son, "Bring me another vessel." And he said to
her, "There is not another vessel." So the oil ceased."*

2 Kings 4:26

In 2 Kings 4, the prophet Elisha gives a word to a childless couple. As a result of the couple's kindness toward Elisha, the Lord gave them a son. You know the story. The son became ill and died. The mother sought the prophet but as she went, her statement to everyone who asked was, "All is well". In other words, "I see what's before me but my testimony of faith is, everything is alright."

Some of you may be looking at situations and circumstances that appear to be anything but all right. However, I have come to meet you where you are and to prophesy into your situation that, "All is well!" Speak to the dead things around you and command them to live. God is not dead and neither are the promises He's made unto you! Though the vision tarry (takes its time to arrive) it shall surely come to pass! Use the faith you have to believe. "It is so," says the Lord of Hosts and the hosts of warring angelic beings are fighting for you.

Command this day to restore and release what belongs to you! Then you too, as the Shunammite woman can reply, "Everything is alright."

# Devotion 76:
# Alignment

*"Behold, You desire truth in the inward parts, and in
the hidden part You will make me to know wisdom.
Purge me with hyssop, and I shall be clean; Wash me,
and I shall be whiter than snow."*

Psalm 51:6-7

While driving into the city one morning, for
some reason I released the steering wheel
to check the alignment of the car's front
end. Back in my youth, although my father didn't drive,
he once told me that if I released the steering wheel and
the car pulled to either the left or right the car's front
end was probably out of alignment. So, for years I've
done that simple alignment test. In every instance, if
the car veered from its path, my father's advice proved
to be true.

Sometimes we need to check our spiritual
alignment. As we communicate with the Lord through
prayer, fasting, worship, fellowship with other believers
and hearing the preached word of God, we can be
assured that our alignment with Him and His will for
our lives are on the right path. Although there may
be detours and delays along the way, low tire pressure
because we fail to keep our suspension system properly
sustained through the aforementioned methods, and

even involuntary pulling of our life in ways we do not wish, we can be fully restored to the right path by returning for maintenance found in the arms of the Savior. Every time we utilized the service men of faith, patience, expectations, trust in God and application of His word, we get a complete overhaul of our misaligned front end. We then come out as if we just came off the dealer's showroom floor, spanking brand new.

You don't discard a vehicle because it's out of alignment. You take it in for repair. God doesn't discard us either. Don't allow anyone to discard you nor do you discard yourself. Come in for repair. The overhaul may initially be met with resistance but the final product is a perfectly aligned vehicle ready for use by the Maker Himself.

Other Verses: Psalm 51:1-13

 **Devotion 77:**
**Never Alone**

*"Teaching them to observe all things that I have commanded you; and lo, I am with you always, even to the end of the age." Amen.*

Matthew 28:20

When I stop and listen I can hear the sound of the abundance of rain. When I take time to focus I can see the shift that is happening in my life. When I give reverence to the voice that is whispering within I can walk without fear of what's ahead. For I can hear a voice behind me gently saying, "This is the way walk in it."

I can see the outstretched arms of the Savior providing both sanctity and rest. He bids me to come. He guides me by His Spirit. He provides an open channel of communication. Nothing ever changes on His part. I am always first on His agenda! I am always His top priority! His love for me never ceases nor changes. He loves me with an everlasting love. He doesn't turn His back on me nor ignore my cry. He's always near. He's always attentive. If there is a breakdown in communication, the breakdown doesn't lie in Him. So I must evaluate the seeming absence of

His presence as to when I turned from Him because my Father and Lord will never turn His back on me. He promised never to leave me. The question I must ask is, "Have I walked away from Him?"

 **Devotion 78:
Love**

*"Though I speak with the tongues of men and of
angels, but have not love, I have become sounding
brass or a clanging cymbal."*

1 Corinthians 13:1

Tina Turner asked the question, "What's love
got to do with it?" The Apostle Paul gives the
answer in 1 Corinthians 13. Without love you
are as sounding brass or a tinkling cymbal. I believe
James Brown paraphrased that to say, "you're talking
loud and saying nothing." Love is full of action. Love
puts a demand on us to have compassion on others.
God's love beckons us to step forward and correct the
injustices a disillusioned society has placed on people
of all races, nationalities, and ethnic groups.

Love provides the response to the question but only
as you and I give it out as freely as it was given to us
by our Lord. It's been shed abroad in our hearts. Love
never fails. Love causes us to forgive time and time
again. As we go about today, we must be conscious that
there's someone crossing our path asking the question,
"Where is the love you promised me?" Don't be afraid
to give love away. Love is and always will be the greatest
gift we have to present.

Other Verses: 1 Corinthians 13:1-13

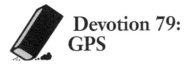

# Devotion 79:
# GPS

*"Your word is a lamp to my feet and a light to my path."*

Psalm 119:105

Over the bridge, make a sharp right onto East 3rd. Then immediately turn right on to Logan. In 325 yards, make a right turn onto Main Street. In 175 yards Main Street will become East College. In 1/2 mile turn right onto North Edgar Street. Stay on Edgar for 3/4 a mile. Your destination will be on the left. You are arriving at your destination.

Twists and turns are all apart of the travel route we call life. In unfamiliar circumstances, we need a good GPS we can rely upon. Isn't it wonderful that we have the word of God to be a light to our paths and lamp to our feet? When we hit dark places we have the illumination of His word to let us see what may be ahead Isn't it a blessing to have the Holy Spirit whispering to us each step of the way? Always guiding us into the will and perfect way of God so should we miss a turn, because we were going too fast or we're not focused on the route, He gently recalculates and puts us back on track. The original GPS is God's Word and the Holy Spirit. Move over OnStar we have a better system in place.

Other Verses: John 14:26

# Devotion 80:
# Run The Race

*"I have fought the good fight, I have finished the race,*
*I have kept the faith."*

2 Timothy 4:7-8

If the race of life was only a run on a straight stretch with an occasional curve to turn, the race wouldn't be so difficult to complete. However, the race we're in has hurdles we must jump over, lanes we must stay in and people on either side of us running at a speed that either sets our pace or causes us to over exert ourselves trying to keep up.

Since we know there is a prize at the finish line (that is nowhere in sight) we press on seeking by faith to obtain a prize that we've longed for since the revelation of eternal life was revealed to us. At times it seems we've barely cleared one hurdle before there's another and the persons on either side keep bumping into us or cutting into our lanes. Nevertheless, we press on. The prize we must obtain isn't carnal or of earthen origin. It beckons for us and pulls us toward the finish line each day.

So, forgetting those things which are behind, we press toward the prize of the high call we have been chosen to answer. We run with determination. We run in faith. We run through the pain associated with the race we're in. We clear every obstacle. This race we shall complete because we run in faith and with patience. We run knowing our expected end shall surely include a robe of righteousness, a crown of glory, and the announcement by our Lord, "Well done! Thy good and faithful servant!" Well don't just sit there. Get up. We've got a race to run.

Other Verses: Philippians 3:14

# Devotion 81:
# All The Glory

*"To whom be glory forever and ever. Amen."*

Galatians 1:5

To God be the glory for the things He has done! To give recognition to anyone else negates the power of the One who has always kept and cared for us. To keep silent reflects a heart of ingratitude. From dangers seen and unseen, He has protected us. From the darkest night and through the gloomiest day He has brought us. From the mess and mire and seemingly bottomless pit, He has pulled us. One step at a time, He has led us. One meal at a time, He has fed us. In the good times and the bad times having Him there made the difference.

If we had ten thousand tongues we would not be able to say "thank you" enough for all He's done for us. However, through our lives we can live a life that reflects His grace, mercy, peace, and His nature of love. Doing this correlates with and substantiates our verbal declaration of "To God be the glory!" His word for our lives is established!

Now out of the mouths of two or three let us too establish what He has done. As well as who He is to each of us. Speaking out of our own mouths let us tell someone where He's brought us from, how He's preserved our souls, and what a mighty God He's been in our lives. With every declaration we exemplify His creative power at work in our lives. In unison, let us all say, "To God be the glory!" Amen!

# Devotion 82:
# Your Timing

*"Wait on the Lord; Be of good courage, and He shall strengthen your heart; Wait, I say, on the Lord!"*

Psalm 27:14

I was awakened one morning by the sound of the alarm in the apartment next door, and I immediately started to gather my bearings. Oh my, I'm late! At least that was my first thought. Then I realized it wasn't my alarm that was sounding and that it wasn't time for me to start moving about. Case in point, sometimes we move ahead of our schedule. We know all the right things, have all the necessary tools, have access to the appropriate network to be successful but the alarm that's sounding does not belong to us.

Stop. Your time is coming. Moving ahead at the sound of someone else's alarm clock puts you on the road too soon. Out of sync, you'll arrive at your destination way ahead of schedule and possibly not be ready for what's ahead. For your assignment, you need to be on time at your appointed time. So listen to the voice within that aligns itself with the timing of God. This alarm awakens you to move about at the time where your labor won't be in vain, your burden will be light, and the yoke will be easy. Get in place to hear so you can move in the rhythm of your timing not the person next door.

Other Verses: Isaiah 40:31

# Devotion 83:
# Child Of God

*"The next day John saw Jesus coming toward him,
and said, "Behold! The Lamb of God who takes away
the sin of the world!"*

John 1:29

I keep hearing the words to a song that Arielle, my daughter forwarded me some time ago. The words say, "I'm no longer a slave to sin. I am a child of God." Meditate on that for a few minutes. Doesn't the knowledge of whose child you are add relevance to your current situation? Doesn't knowing this truth produce energy that was missing just a minute before? Aren't you even now beginning to see life in a different perspective?

You are a child of the omnipotent Father; an offspring of the omniscient Master; a descendant of the omnipresent King! You've been freed from sin by the blood of the slain Lamb of God. John said, "Behold the Lamb of God who takes away the sin of the world." You're a child of the Most High God! There is no one greater! What a revelation to fully grasp! Say it aloud with boldness and clarity. "I am a child of God!" As often as needed remind yourself, "I'm no longer a slave to sin. I am a child of God."

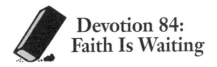

# Devotion 84:
# Faith Is Waiting

*"Therefore do not cast away your confidence,*
*which has great reward."*

Hebrews 10:35

When questions are asked of others and the final answers given, you have to be ready to accept the response. However, when you are questioned and must give the answer, it's up to you to give the response. Whether your reply is fact or fiction, you determine the response. Now today the question is, "Where is your faith?" I cannot answer for you nor be judgmental of your reply. The critical issue is, "Will you be honest with yourself?" If so, the opportunity to go forth is greater than ever before.

Don't waste the opportunity. Faith is ready to move for you. Don't throw it away in disappointment or leave it on the shelf of unbelief. Faith stands tall when the demand is placed on it. Have confidence in Him. He doesn't waiver. If you've put faith down, turn around, go back to the place where you left it, and grab hold to it in earnest expectation of the results you've been promised. Faith is waiting to move but it's in your response.

Other Verses: Luke 8:25

# Devotion 85:
# Look At The Heart

*"But the Lord said to Samuel, "Do not look at his appearance or at his physical stature, because I have refused him. For the Lord does not see as man sees; for man looks at the outward appearance, but the Lord looks at the heart."*

1 Samuel 16:7

What would happen if before we saw an individual's physical attributes we saw their heart? Would we be so quick to become judgmental? Would we really want to be just like him or her? Would we truly desire to run into his arms because "He's so fine!", or "She's just what I've always wanted!" What if their face was just a blur and all you knew to recognize them was their voice?

When you finally saw them face to face would it even matter what their appearance was because your first impression was the lasting impression based on the content of their heart? Remember God told Samuel as he was searching for a king among Jessie's sons, "You're looking at the outward appearance but I'm looking at the heart." Out of the heart flows life or death. The mouth only speaks what's in the heart. Perhaps we should spend less time looking at people to determine their value or worth and instead listen to the pureness of their hearts.

# Devotion 86:
# Become Friendly

*"A man who has friends must himself be friendly, but
there is a friend who sticks closer than a brother."*

Proverbs 18:24

Do know how you have friends on Facebook that you really don't know? Well, one morning I met a friend from Facebook that I didn't know. The odd thing about this meeting is that most mornings, we're both standing at the Exxon coffee counter getting coffee side-by-side. One morning, she read my name tag and told me who she was. We chatted for a while and went our separate ways. Oddly enough, as we drove past one another we waved and smiled as if we'd known each other for a lifetime.

Who's standing next to you that you know but you really don't know? The man you walk past holding a sign asking for food may be an angel waiting to see how you'll respond. The woman who's stranded on the side of the road could have a word for you. The child who's having a meltdown at the Family Dollar may only need you to say hello. The person standing beside you at the coffee counter just might have the conversation that ignites a lasting friendship. Don't you think it's time you took notice and introduce yourself? The next time you meet someone, become fully aware of the person standing before you. You have nothing to lose. Show yourself to be friendly.

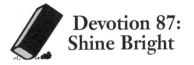

# Devotion 87:
# Shine Bright

*"Let your light so shine before men, that they may see your good works and glorify your Father in heaven."*

Matthew 5:16

We don't have to be a star to be in God's show. However, we will shine. In our leading role as ambassadors to the nations, we'll go forth proclaiming the good news of the gospel. We'll go correcting the injustices imputed upon mankind, laying hands on the sick that they may be healed, and releasing the anointing to set free any and all who are bound. Yes. It's true. We don't have to be a star. However, like the moon is a star that reflects light from the sun, we are a reflection of God's Son. We shall be seen! Yet, unlike the moon there should be no waning or decreasing of His image. Until His work in us is complete, we continue to grow until we reach the completed work He has begun in us. Until then, we shine bright.

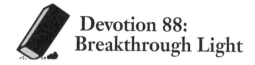

# Devotion 88:
# Breakthrough Light

*"The entrance of Your words gives light; It gives understanding to the simple."*

Psalm 119:130

See the light in the midst of the dark clouds? Focus on the light. Darkness may hover around but in the light is where you're destined to be. God's word brings illumination to darkness. Focus on His word. In the light of His word, you'll find tranquility. You'll discover rest. You'll uncover passion, purpose, plenty, and the plan for your life. Breakthrough today is not just in the clouds. Breakthrough for you is found in the light of God's word. So in my Jenny from Forrest Gump voice, "Run, Forrest, Run!" Run to the light!

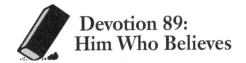

# Devotion 89:
# Him Who Believes

*"Jesus said to him, "If you can believe, all things are possible to him who believes."*

Mark 9:23

D o you have faith to believe what you desire most from God? If not, are your desires directed in the wrong direction? If so, are you willing to go in the direction His purpose will direct you? What you believe ultimately determines your level of faith to act. Today, stop and reflect on your belief system. Don't allow your beliefs to hinder the pull of faith to the next level of action needed for you to be a dominating force to reckon with in your assignment. Actually, if the truth be told, your belief may be unbelief (Mark 9:23-24) in action. Let faith in God consume your thought processes. Through prayer and fasting your desires become God's desires and you shall have the desires of your heart.

Other Scriptures: Mark 9:14-29

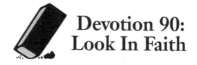 **Devotion 90:**
**Look In Faith**

*"Now faith is the substance of things hoped for, the evidence of things not seen."*

Hebrews 11:1

Some days clouds are hanging low and are somewhat dark. As they move at a relatively slow pace, on the horizon you can see a break in the dark to lighter less intimidating clouds. Dark clouds remind us of the turbulence and possible storm that's coming. Yet should we pay close enough attention we'll find that the dark clouds are slowly but surely moving away and light is on the horizon.

As in nature, so goes the same in our lives. The situation may look bleak. The circumstance may appear at a stalemate. The problem seem stagnant. Yet, if we look closer, we too shall see that things are moving. Stagnant doesn't mean forever. Stalemate doesn't infer a fresh start can't happen. Bleak doesn't imply dismal has taken residence.

Now is the time to look through the eyes of faith. Faith sees what we can't. Faith knows that all things are working for our good so it just sees the end results. Clouds pass in the natural. So shall the storms of life we face. We may be standing in a storm but if we look in faith we can clearly see the light on the horizon. This too shall pass.

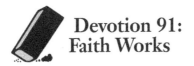

# Devotion 91:
# Faith Works

*"But do you want to know, O foolish man, that faith without works is dead?"*

James 2:20

Faith without works is dead. I've said this already, didn't I? There's more to say. Although faith is a noun, it is also an action word. What I mean by this is faith is present to work for you. Left lying dormant, like muscles that are not used faith becomes weak, placid and eventually doesn't work at all. For this reason you must call up the force of faith and allow it to cover you as faith works diligently to handle your business for you. Faith is more than willing to work and anxiously anticipates you to put a demand on him. Faith is ready, willing, and able to move mountains for you. What would you have faith to do?

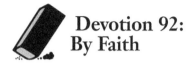 **Devotion 92:
By Faith**

*"By faith they passed through the Red Sea as by dry land, whereas the Egyptians, attempting to do so, were drowned."*

Hebrews 11: 29

Faith without works is dead. Faith is your servant. He activates what has already been promised to you. He's the catalyst you need, the boost you've been wanting, the stimulus you've been seeking, and the impetus you've overlooked.

Haven't received a promise from God yet? Check to see if you've put faith to work or if you've set him to the side. Where is your faith? He just might be taking an extended coffee break because you've failed to call him back to work. Speak to your faith just like you do everything else.

We are people of great faith. Exercise your faith and let your name be added to the Faith Hall of Fame. I can see it now, "By faith, Vera walked boldly into her wealthy place unscathed by the enemy!" Put faith to work for you. Attention! Faith! Arise! You've got work to do!

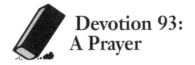 # Devotion 93:
## A Prayer

*"Create in me a clean heart, O God, and renew a steadfast spirit within me."*

Psalm 51:10

et's say this together, "Today Lord, I open my heart to you. Come inside. Repair its broken valves. Restore a constant flow of your healing. Remove the hurt I should have let go of years ago. Renew your love to flow freely from it. Thank you Father. I receive all that I've asked for in the name of Jesus. I give you the glory as I demonstrate the healing that has taken place in my heart on today. Amen."

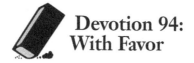

# Devotion 94:
# With Favor

*"For You, O Lord, will bless the righteous; With favor
You will surround him as with a shield."*

Psalm 5:12

What a beautiful weekend for graduates, mothers, and people across the globe! Families united and celebrated with one another. Joyful memories were released into the timeless expanse of the universe. Today's a new day filled with the expectations of greatness and gladness. The time has come for the week to begin and we do so with the anticipatory mindset of God's glory and grace going before us. With His favor encompassing us, His love overshadowing us and His blood covering us we are blessed. We've lived the weekend and now we're ready for the week ahead. All hearts clear? Then let's go! We've got an assignment to complete one day at a time. Today's our day to make a mark. It's our time. Blessed and sanctified is the service we'll render! Wealth and riches we'll receive. To glory be glory! Amen!

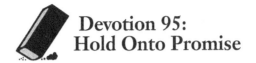# Devotion 95:
## Hold Onto Promise

*"Now faith is the substance of things hoped for, the evidence of things not seen."*

Hebrews 11:1

When I received an Education Specialist degree, I was in a non-threatening environment. However, the grip I had on this diploma cover was as if it was for dear life. I'm holding on to it as if to say "Want a fight? Then just try and take it from me." Now this same stance you too must take when the enemy tries to take what God has promised you.

He has no right to what you're entitled to by the blood of Jesus. What's more, you must hold on in faith. You see the degree isn't in the cover. It's going to be mailed. By faith I'm holding the cover because I've met the requirements to possess the documentation of the promise. So the promise you have, though it's not yet in your possession, hold on as if you had it in your hands. Don't let go! Your faith is the entitlement to the promise and the evidence that it shall surely come.

 **Devotion 96:
A New Day**

*"Do not remember the former things, nor consider the things of old. Behold, I will do a new thing, now it shall spring forth; Shall you not know it? I will even make a road in the wilderness and rivers in the desert."*

Isaiah 43:18-19

Today's a new day. It's filled with opportunities that weren't present on yesterday. Today has open doors that were closed yesterday. Today offers a second chance. Today gives us a different view of what was seen yesterday. Today is a new day.

Wow! Sometimes all you really need to know is that today is a new day. Without any input from anyone else, today gives us a new outlook on old circumstances. Today provides a fresh view of stale decisions.

The former things are in the past and newness awaits you. Today there is no need to dwell on yesterday's mistakes nor anticipate tomorrow's obstacles. Just live in today and let today be all that it is destined to be. Today's a new day! It belongs to you. Smile! Today's your new day.

# Devotion 97:
## God Has You

*"Because you have made the Lord, who is my refuge,*
*even the Most High, your dwelling place, no evil*
*shall befall you, Nor shall any plague come near your*
*dwelling; For He shall give His angels charge over*
*you, to keep you in all your ways."*

Psalm 91:9-11

Everyone who grew up in the country or ever rode in the front seat with your granny or mother through rural Dallas County at night will know exactly what I'm talking about. One night while traveling back from Sparkman on Arkansas Hwy 273 (through the bottoms) around 9:30 p.m., as usual the highway was lined with deer grazing under the full moon. As I neared the Hopeville area two large does (female deer) decided to cross the road in front of me.

Immediately, involuntarily, simultaneously with braking, my right arm reached across to soften the impact (should it occur) of Arielle, the passenger sitting beside me. As I reached across her body I heard myself whisper, "It's okay. I got you." She never flinched or braced herself. She just smiled and watched as the deer sauntered across In front of the vehicle.

Case in point: what you're going through today, just listen and you'll hear the whisper of the voice of the Holy Spirit saying, "It's okay. I got you." Like Arielle, don't flinch or brace yourself, just smile and watch the problem dissipate. God is strategically moving for you this day. Relax and let Him have His way! All things, including "your current situation", is working for your good! You're sheltered and protected by the Lord God Almighty!

# Devotion 98:
# We Win

*"And you, being dead in your trespasses and the uncircumcision of your flesh, He has made alive together with Him, having forgiven you all trespasses, having wiped out the handwriting of requirements that was against us, which was contrary to us. And He has taken it out of the way, having nailed it to the cross. Having disarmed principalities and powers, He made a public spectacle of them, triumphing over them in it."*

Colossians 2:13-15

Excuse me, Devil! Your words are merely lies and are not the responses I was expecting. So let's get this straight. I am blessed, highly favored by God, and no longer subject to the fallacies you've brought before me as fact. I live in the overflow of perfect health, overwhelming prosperity, and abundant living. I am happy! I am healed of all past hurts, fears, and doubts.

No is not the answer I accept unless I choose to do so. I'm not afraid! I'm not sorry! I'm not backing down! You started this fight but I'm finishing it. Don't turn tail and run now devil, the fight is on! Like Liam Neeson in the action thriller movie, Taken, I have a particular set of skills. I'm going to find you and I'm going to annihilate your every assault. Devil, your reign is over. In fact, it ended at Calvary! What part of get out don't you understand? The adjective applied to your name is defeated. This kingdom belongs to God Almighty. It suffers violence and we take it by force.

Ready or not here I come. God is fighting for me, pushing back the darkness, raising up the Kingdom that cannot be shaken. In the name of Jesus, the enemy is defeated and we will shout it out! We Win! Hallelujah!

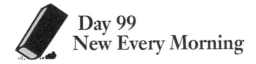

# Day 99
## New Every Morning

*"This I recall to my mind, therefore I have hope.*
*Through the Lord's mercies we are not consumed,*
*because His compassions fail not. They are new every*
*morning; Great is Your faithfulness."*

Lamentations 3:21-23

Think of a time you were forgiven by someone. Oh, what a relief it was to have mercy shown! After all you'd committed the offense and you weren't sure if you'd be reconciled back into your original position. Yet, as you sought with a pure heart, forgiveness was granted. Now just like as in the natural so in the spirit. Our Father has forgiven us of all our past, present, and future mistakes. It is by His grace and mercy that we aren't consumed. Because His compassion doesn't fail and His loving kindness is renewed every morning, we are at liberty to draw from His great faithfulness every day of our lives.

We are God's masterpiece created in the image of His dear son. Inside us dwells His Holy Spirit who leads us into righteousness, if we but harken to His voice. When justice should have been served, mercy stood up and pleaded our case. The faithful God showed compassion and our guilty verdict was overturned by the blood of Jesus. Suffering the humility of the cross for us, Jesus reconciled and redeemed us back into the royal priesthood of God's Kingdom. Hence, today we stand as kings and priests, clothed in righteousness, washed in His blood, and all stains of sins past, present, and future erased.

How can we not stand in awe of such great love? How can we not bow in submission to such endearing compassion? Looking beyond our faults, God sees our needs. Each day, all day He grants unto us His hand of grace and mercy. Today is no exception. Whatever you need from Him, His hand is extended as you seek His face. So we pray, "Lord, we seek Your face. Show us Your will for us today. We know that as we handle Your affairs, you supply everything we need to reign as kings and priests in Your ministry of reconciliation to others. Thank You for redeeming us and granting us another chance to spread the good news of the gospel. Glory to Your name! Amen."

Other Verses: Ephesians 2:1-11